MY
PARTY
BOOK

MY PARTY BOOK

Marion Elliot
Cheryl Owen

Little, Brown and Company
Boston New York Toronto London

First North American Edition 1995

ISBN 0-316-77114-7

Library of Congress Catalog Card Number 94-76968

Produced by Salamander Books Limited,
129-137 York Way, London N7 9LG, England

10 9 8 7 6 5 4 3 2 1

CREDITS

Editor: Helen Stone
Designer: Rachael Stone
Photographer: Jonathon Pollock
Illustrator: Teri Gower
Character illustrator: Jo Gapper
Diagram artist: Malcolm Porter
Additional material by: Dennis Patten
Crafts inspector: Leslie Thompson
Color separation by: P & W Graphics, Pte., Singapore

Published simultaneously in Canada by
Little, Brown & Company (Canada) Limited.

Printed in Italy

CONTENTS

INTRODUCTION

Everybody loves the fun and excitement of a party. Whether you are the host or a guest, there is nothing quite like the sight of decorations and party goodies to get you in the mood to celebrate. *My Party Book* **is packed with exciting things to make — from cards, hats, masks, and decorations to treats to eat and games to play. All of the projects are clearly explained, easy to do, and sure to make your party a hit.**

BEFORE YOU BEGIN

● Check with an adult before starting any project; you might need some help.

● Read the instructions all the way through before you begin a project.

● Start by gathering together all the things you will need.

● Cover your work surface with newspaper or an old cloth.

● Protect your clothes by wearing an apron or by covering up with an old shirt.

WHEN YOU HAVE FINISHED

● Put everything away. Pens, glue, paints, and other materials can be stored in old boxes, cookie tins, or ice cream containers.

● Wash out any paintbrushes, and remember to put the lids back on pens, paints, and glue containers.

SAFETY FIRST

Use common sense when working with anything sharp or hot. You will be able to make most of the projects in this book by yourself, but sometimes you will need the help of an adult. Keep an eye out for the SAFETY TIPS. They appear on those projects with which you'll need help. When you have finished making decorations, ask an adult to put them up for you.

Please remember the basic rules of safety:

● Never leave scissors open or lying around where smaller children can reach them.

● Always stick needles or pins into a pincushion or scrap of cloth when you are not using them.

● Never use an oven, sharp scissors, or a craft knife without the help or supervision of an adult.

Be very careful when using sharp knives and scissors.

Get everything ready before you start, and don't forget to clean up afterward!

USING PATTERNS

At the back of the book, you will find the patterns you will need to make many of the projects in this book. Using a pencil and tracing paper, trace the pattern you need. Turn your tracing over and place it facedown on the card or paper you are using for the design. Hold the paper firmly in place, and trace over the pencil lines. When you take the tracing paper away, the pattern will be left on the card and ready to cut out.

Once you have gained confidence making some of the projects in this book, you can go on to create your own designs.

GROWN-UPS TAKE NOTE

Every project in *My Party Book* has been designed to be simple to make, with satisfying results. However, some potentially dangerous items such as a craft knife, wire, oven, or kitchen utensils are needed for some of the projects. Your involvement will depend on the age and ability of the child. We recommend that you read through any project in this book before it is undertaken.

MATERIALS AND EQUIPMENT

Each project has a list of everything you need to make it. You may already have many of these things at home, but check with an adult before you take anything. Set aside a box to collect scraps of wrapping paper, cereal boxes, tubes from paper towel or toilet paper rolls, and other household packing that can be reused.

If you have a sewing basket at home, ask if you can hunt through it for scraps of ribbon, sequins, beads, and buttons. Additional items such as modeling clay, glitter, crepe paper, and craft varnish can be bought from craft shops or stationery stores.

When making the food and drink projects, be sure that all your ingredients are fresh and that your utensils and work surface are clean. Prepare your food as near to party time as possible, and cover it or wrap it up well before storing it in a cool, clean place.

Never use a craft knife or oven without the help of an adult.

CROWNING GLORIES

These impressive-looking crowns, decorated with colorful pasta shapes, will transform you into the king or queen of the party. If you don't have any pasta, try using dried beans or pumpkin and melon seeds instead.

YOU WILL NEED

Colored card stock
Scissors
Pencil; ruler
Tracing paper
All-purpose glue
Paper clips
Dried pasta shapes
Poster paints
Paintbrush

3 Paint the pasta shapes in bright colors, and leave them to dry. You can create different patterns by using an assortment of pasta shapes. Follow the designs here or make up your own.

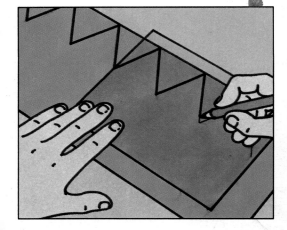

1 Cut out a 24-inch by 4-inch strip of colored card stock. Using the pencil and ruler, draw three or four connecting triangles on tracing paper. Turn the tracing paper facedown on your strip of card stock, and trace over the pencil lines to transfer the design onto the top edge of the card. Move the tracing paper along, and repeat this step until the zigzags run the length of your card strip. Cut them out.

2 If you wish, curl the points of your crown by bending them over the pencil. Wrap the crown around your head to find the right size. Glue the overlapped ends of your crown together. Hold the ends together with paper clips until the glue has dried.

4 Glue the painted pasta shapes to the crown in rows or patterns. Don't use too much pasta, or the crown will be too heavy to wear.

BEAUTIFUL BUTTERFLY MASKS

You will be the belle of the ball wearing one of these elegant butterfly-shaped masks. You can decorate your mask as simply or as lavishly as you like. Sequins, feathers, beads, and glitter can be used to add an extra touch of sparkly glamour. Hold your mask up to your face as you greet your guests to start your party with an air of mystery.

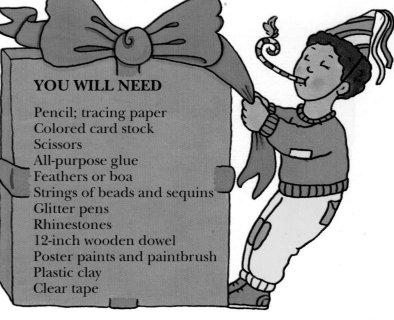

YOU WILL NEED

Pencil; tracing paper
Colored card stock
Scissors
All-purpose glue
Feathers or boa
Strings of beads and sequins
Glitter pens
Rhinestones
12-inch wooden dowel
Poster paints and paintbrush
Plastic clay
Clear tape

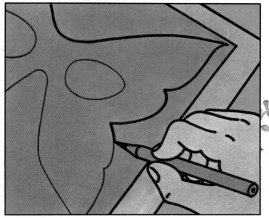

1 Using the pencil and tracing paper, trace the butterfly mask pattern on page 82. Lay the tracing paper facedown on the colored card stock. Trace over the pencil lines to transfer the shape onto the card stock. Cut out the mask.

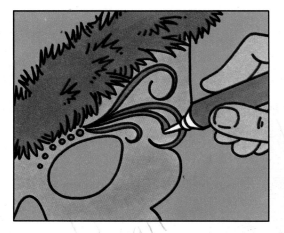

3 Glue strings of beads or sequins in patterns onto the mask. Continue decorating the mask by drawing designs with glitter pens and by gluing on rhinestones.

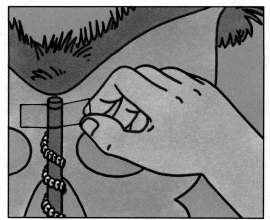

4 Paint the wooden dowel, and push one end into some plastic clay to hold it while it dries. When it's dry, wrap the dowel with a string of beads, gluing the bead string in place at each end of the dowel. Glue the dowel to the back of your mask either at one side or in the center, as shown, and secure it with clear tape.

2 Glue some feathers upright behind the mask, or glue a length of boa along the top edge.

PAPER CHAINS

A party wouldn't be the same without pretty paper chains for decoration. Store-bought ones can be expensive, and besides, it's much more fun to make your own at home.

1 To make looped paper chains, cut strips of colored paper measuring about 6 inches long by 1 inch wide. Fold one strip into a loop, and staple or glue the ends together. Thread the next strip through the first loop, and glue as shown. Continue in this way to make a long chain.

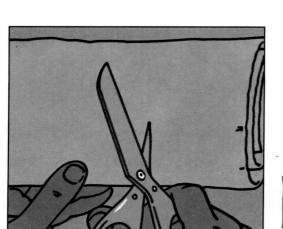

2 To make simple crepe paper twists, cut a 3-inch-wide band from the end of a roll of double-sided crepe paper. Unravel the roll to make a long ribbon of paper.

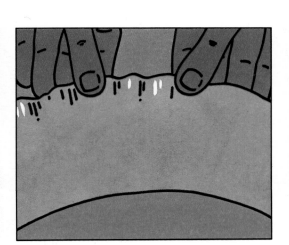

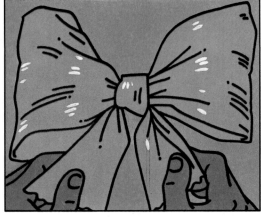

3 Gently pinch along both edges of the ribbon, pulling gently to form a wavy edge. Ask an adult to hang the strip for you, attaching one end to the wall with tape and twisting the ribbon several times before attaching the other end farther along the wall.

4 Beautiful bows can be made from twisted paper ribbon. Cut a length of ribbon about 18 inches long. Unroll the ribbon, smoothing it out into a flat strip. Fold both ends into the center, and staple or glue them in place.

5 Cut a second length of ribbon 10 inches long, and unravel it as before. Pinch the original paper in the center, and tie the shorter length around it to form a bow. To finish, cut a V shape out of each end of the binding ribbon.

LUCKY DIP FISH

A gentle nudge has this shimmering fish rocking to and fro as though swimming in the sea. Fill it with shredded tissue paper, and hide small gifts inside to make a stunning lucky dip for your party guests.

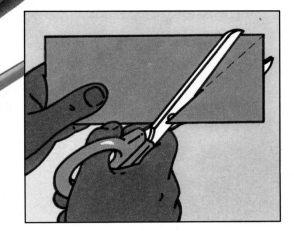

3 To make the fins, cut out two rectangles of metallic crepe paper. Cut off one end of each fin diagonally, and scrunch up the straight end. Glue one fin to each side of the fish.

1 Cut the sides from the large corrugated cardboard box. On one of the side pieces, draw a large oval bigger than the sides of the smaller box. Cut the oval out. Lay the oval on the other side piece, draw around it, and cut out a second oval. Glue the ovals to opposite sides of the small box.

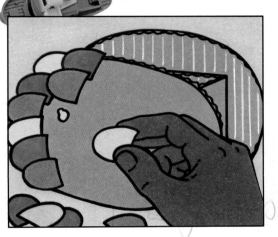

2 Paint the small box and the ovals with pearlized paint. Cut out some scales from metallic crepe paper. Starting at one end, glue the scales on the ovals in overlapping rows. Glue on buttons for eyes. Cut a mouth from red metallic crepe paper, and glue it on.

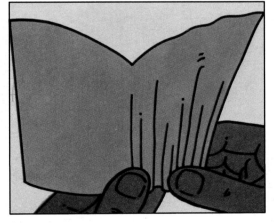

4 For the tails, cut four squares of crepe paper 8 inches by 8 inches. Glue two of the squares together, back-to-back. Glue the last two squares together as well. Cut a V shape out of one side of each glued-together square, and scrunch together the opposite side. Glue the tails to the back of the fish, one on the undecorated side of each oval. Fill the box with shredded tissue paper and small gifts.

TWIRLING BOW TIES

YOU WILL NEED

Pencil; tracing paper
Colored card stock
Scissors; colored paper
Glue stick
Craft knife (for
   adult use only)
Bottle cork
Paper fastener
Large button or bottle top
All-purpose glue
Large plastic-covered paper
   clip

Wearing one of these smart novelty bow ties will get you noticed at any party. Clip one on to your collar, give it a gentle push, and amaze party guests as your tie spins around and around. Choose your own decorations or follow the designs here.

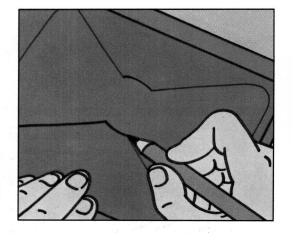

1 Using the pencil and tracing paper, trace the bow tie pattern on page 83. Lay the tracing paper facedown on the colored card stock, and trace over the pencil lines to transfer the shape onto the card stock. Cut the bow tie shape out.

2 Cut out decorations such as spots or stripes from colored paper, and glue these to your bow tie using the glue stick.

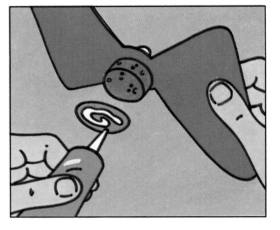

5 Place the large button or the bottle top on some colored card stock. Draw around it, and cut out the circle. Glue the circle to the back of the cork.

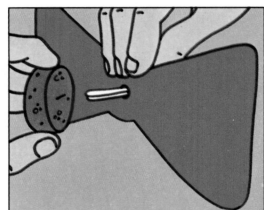

3 Ask an adult to use the craft knife to cut a piece from the bottle cork about 1/2 inch thick and to make a small hole through its center.

4 Use the paper fastener to make a small hole in the center of the bow tie. Push the paper fastener through the bow tie and into the hole in the cork. The fastener should not stick out the back of the cork, and the bow tie should spin freely.

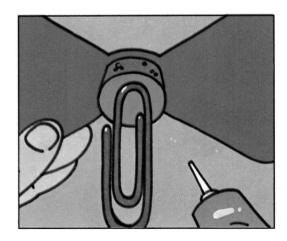

6 Using the all-purpose glue, glue the large paper clip to the back of the cork. When the glue is dry, simply clip your bow tie onto your collar.

SAFETY TIP: *Make sure an adult helps you when using a craft knife.*

SPOOKY NAPKIN RINGS

These spooky napkin rings will add the finishing touch to the table at a Halloween party, alongside jack-o'-lanterns and a witch's brew punch. You could also use them to hold together bundles of candy sticks or lollipops as trick-or-treat gifts.

YOU WILL NEED

Pencil; tracing paper
Black and orange card stock
Scissors; ruler
Toilet paper tube
Green poster paint
Paintbrush
All-purpose glue
Thick green pipe cleaner
2 black beads
Scrap of red paper

1 To make the bat napkin ring, trace the pattern on page 83 using the pencil and tracing paper. Lay the tracing facedown on the black card stock. Trace over the outline with a pencil to transfer the shape onto the card stock. Cut out the shape you have drawn, and cut the slits as marked on the pattern. Curl the bat sections around, and slot together as shown.

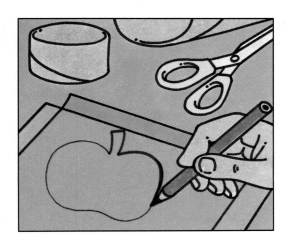

2 To make the pumpkin napkin ring, cut a 1½-inch-wide piece from a toilet paper tube. Paint the ring green, and leave it to dry. Trace the pumpkin pattern from page 83, and transfer the shape onto orange card stock following the instructions in step 1. Cut out the pumpkin, and glue it onto the ring.

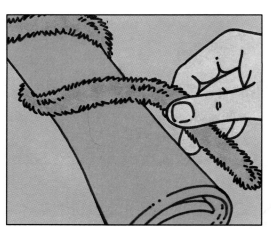

3 To make the snake, wrap a thick pipe cleaner around a rolled napkin. Bend the pipe cleaner ends upward, and glue two black beads to one end for eyes.

4 To complete your snake, cut out a forked tongue from red paper, and glue the end below the eyes as shown.

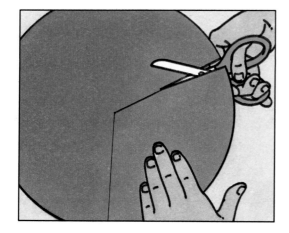

NIGHT AND DAY

These sun and moon hats are great for a party with a night-and-day theme. Some guests could be "night" guests; they could wear pajamas or nightgowns. "Day" guests could wear bright, sunny colors.

1 Using the compass, draw a circle with a 12-inch diameter on blue card stock for the sun hat or on blue metallic card stock for the night hat. Cut the circle out. Cut a slit from the edge of the circle to the pin point in its center, then cut out a piece-of-pie shape, removing about one third of the circle. Bring the two edges together to form a cone. Overlap them slightly, and glue them into place.

YOU WILL NEED
Compass; scissors
Colored and metallic card
  stock
All-purpose glue; clear tape
Hole punch
Narrow gift-wrapping ribbon
Cotton balls
Pencil; tracing paper
Red felt-tip pen
Wire spiral from a notepad
Wire cutters and craft knife
  (for adult use only)
Hat elastic (optional)

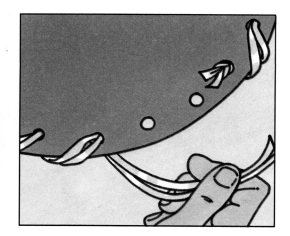

2 Using the hole punch, punch a row of holes around the rim of the hat. Lace two lengths of gift-wrapping ribbon through the holes, gluing the ribbon ends inside the hat at the start and finish. Glue tufts of cotton to the sunshine hat to look like clouds.

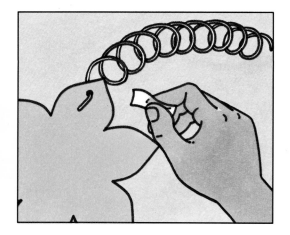

3 Using the pencil and tracing paper, trace the sun, moon, and star patterns on page 83. Lay the sun and star tracings facedown on yellow card stock, and trace over the outlines to transfer them onto the card stock. Cut out the shapes. Draw a smiling face on the sun. Then ask an adult to cut a 4-inch length of wire. Thread one end of the wire through the sun and the other end into the top of the sun hat. Tape each end in place.

4 Lay the stars you have cut out on top of red, silver, and yellow card stock. Trace around them, and cut out enough stars to decorate the moon hat. Glue them on in a random pattern. Transfer the moon tracing onto silver card stock, and cut out the shape you have drawn. Cut out or draw on an eye. Ask an adult to cut a small slit across the top of the moon hat with a craft knife. Place the moon in the slot.

SAFETY TIP: *Make sure an adult helps you when using wire or a craft knife.*

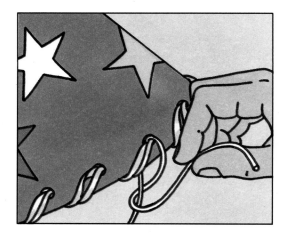

5 If you'd like, you can attach a length of hat elastic to keep your hat in place. Thread each end through a punched hole at either side of your hat, and knot the elastic in place so it fits snugly under your chin when you put your hat on.

ANIMAL GARLANDS

These bold chains will delight animal lovers of all ages. Make the fun chicks or elephants shown here, or adapt the pattern to make your own designs.

YOU WILL NEED

Pencil
Tracing paper
Yellow and orange card stock or pink and white card stock
Scissors
All-purpose glue
Black felt-tip pen

1 Using the pencil and tracing paper, trace the chick or elephant body pattern on page 84. Lay the tracing facedown on the yellow or pink card stock. Trace over the outline to transfer the shape onto the card stock. Repeat this process to make as many chicks or elephants as you need for your garland. Cut them out.

2 Use the process described in step 1 to trace and cut enough elephant ears and tusks or enough beaks to decorate your garland. Glue the top edge of the ears and tusks to the elephants as shown.

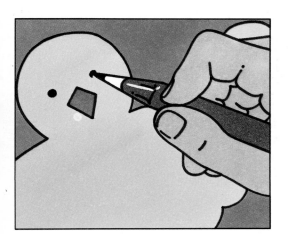

3 Glue the beaks flat onto the center of the chicks' faces. Use a black felt-tip pen to draw on eyes.

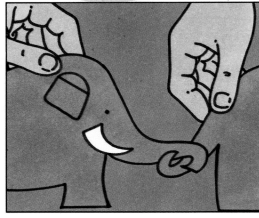

4 Link together the hooked wings of the chicks or the trunks and tails of the elephants. Ask an adult to help you hang your garland.

CIRCUS TENT GOODY BOXES

YOU WILL NEED

Pencil
Tracing paper
Colored card stock
Scissors and ruler
Hole punch
Glitter pens
Small gifts
Cord
Feathers

These gift boxes are easy to make and are an ideal way to present a surprise gift or prize to your guests. They can also be used to wrap small presents to give to friends on their birthdays.

24

1 Using the pencil and tracing paper, trace the circus tent pattern on page 85. Turn your tracing around, and add a third side to your pattern, as shown on the diagram. Lay the tracing facedown on the colored card stock, and trace over the pencil lines to transfer the shape onto the card stock. Cut out the circus tent. Use a scissor blade and the ruler to score along the dotted lines marked on the pattern.

2 Use the hole punch to make a hole in each point of the tent. Decorate the triangular sides of your card shape using glitter pens.

3 Fold the card along the scored lines to form the circus tent shape. Place the gift on the tent base, and bring up the triangular sides to meet, hiding the gift inside.

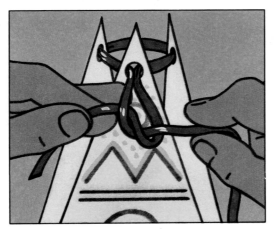

4 Thread a length of cord through each of the punched holes, and fasten the sides together by tying the cord into a bow.

5 Tuck a few brightly colored feathers into the top of the tent for decoration.

DINOSAUR MASKS

Dinosaur fans will love these prehistoric eye masks decorated with their favorite monsters. By adding different shapes cut from crepe paper, you will be able to make an amazing variety of dinosaurs.

YOU WILL NEED

Pencil
Tracing paper
Colored card stock
Scissors
All-purpose glue
Black felt-tip pen
Crepe paper
Dried lentils and split
  peas
Tweezers
Hat elastic

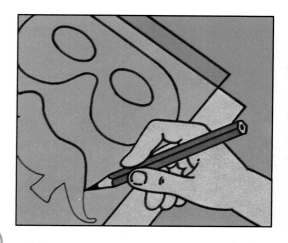

1 Using the pencil and tracing paper, trace the mask, dinosaur body, and triceratops horn patterns on page 86. Lay the tracings facedown on different colored card stock, and trace over the pencil lines to transfer the patterns onto the card stock. Cut out all the shapes you have drawn.

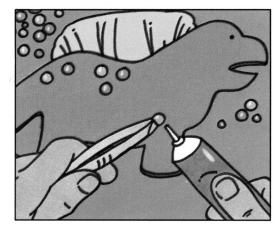

2 Lay the dinosaurs and horns you have cut out onto more card stock. Draw around them, and cut a second set to make matching pairs. Glue the horns behind the triceratops' heads, and draw eyes onto the dinosaurs with a black felt-tip pen.

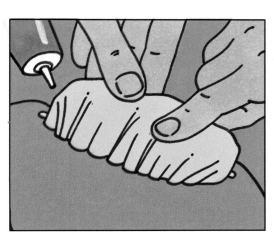

4 Spread a line of glue along the top of the ouranosaurus on the wrong side. Press the long, straight edge of the ruffle onto the glue, bunching up the crepe paper to fit.

5 Using the tweezers for easy handling, glue some lentils and split peas onto the dinosaurs. Sharpen the pencil, and use the point to pierce a hole at the dots on each side of the masks. Thread through a length of elastic, and adjust the length to fit around your head. Knot the ends behind the holes to keep the elastic in place. Glue the dinosaurs onto the masks as shown.

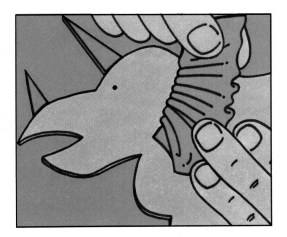

3 Trace the patterns for the triceratops's collar and the ouranosaurus's ruffle on page 86. Follow the instructions in step 1 to cut two of each piece from crepe paper. To attach the collar, spread glue along the dotted line marked on the triceratops pattern. Press the long, straight edge of the collar onto the glue, bunching up the crepe paper to fit.

FLOWER BASKETS

These flowery baskets may look pretty enough to be a gift in themselves, but your party guests are in for a big surprise when they discover that the baskets are also goody bags and have gifts inside, too.

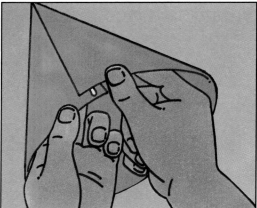

YOU WILL NEED
Compass and pencil
Pink construction paper
Scissors; ruler
All-purpose glue
Clear tape
Artificial flowers and leaves
Crepe paper
Shredded tissue paper
Candy, small soaps,
   or bath beads

1 Using the compass, draw a semicircle 11 inches in diameter on pink construction paper, and cut it out. Bring the edges together so they overlap to make a cone. Glue the edges together. Secure them with clear tape until the glue dries. To make the basket's handle, cut a strip of construction paper ½ inch wide by 11 inches long. Glue each end of the strip inside the cone.

2 Cut off the heads of the artificial flowers (ask an adult to help you if the flowers are fixed on wires). Glue the flowers around the rim of the basket. Glue artificial leaves under the flowers and to the sides of the handle. Smaller flowers can be stuck into any gaps.

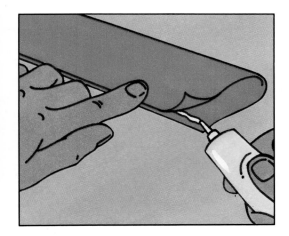

3 To make paper roses, cut 4-inch sections from the end of the crepe paper roll. Open out each strip, and cut a length 19 inches long. Fold the strip in half as shown, without making a sharp crease. Glue the edges together at the bottom.

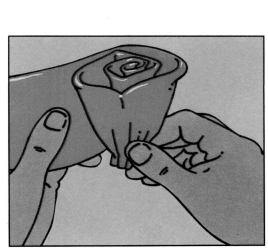

4 Starting at one end, roll up the paper strip, dotting glue along the bottom edge to hold it in place. Make small pleats in the lower edge as you roll, so that the finished rose is not too tight. You need to make about fourteen roses.

5 Glue the roses around the rim of the basket. Cut leaf shapes from green crepe paper, and glue them underneath the roses. Fill the basket with shredded tissue (you can make your own by cutting tissue paper into narrow strips), and put small gifts inside.

SAFETY TIP: *Make sure an adult helps you when using wire.*

PARTY NOISEMAKERS

Noisy toys are great fun at parties, and what could be better than these easy-to-make noisemakers? Hold one corner, give a sharp flick of the wrist, and these simple paper noisemakers make a loud snapping sound. Make lots of them, decorated with potato print designs to suit the theme of your party.

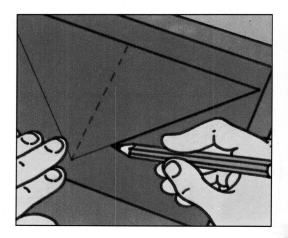

1 Using the pencil and ruler, draw templates for the noisemaker and its insert on tracing paper following the patterns and measurements on page 87. Lay the tracing of the noisemaker facedown on the card stock, and trace over the pencil lines to transfer the shape onto the card stock. Transfer the insert onto thin paper in the same way. Cut out both shapes.

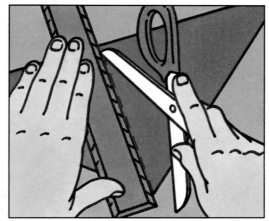

3 Paint the raised design with poster paint, then stamp it onto the noisemaker. Repeat this process to make a pattern, applying more paint to the potato block as necessary.

2 With an adult's help, cut the potato in half, and cut a simple raised design from one half to make a printing block.

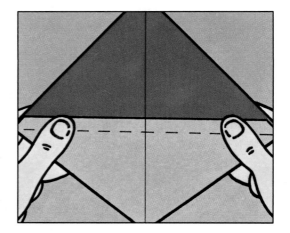

5 Score and fold the noisemaker insert as shown on the pattern. Glue the insert in place along the bottom edge of the open noisemaker, as shown. Fold the insert inside the noisemaker, and allow the glue to dry thoroughly before using.

4 When the paint has dried, use a scissor blade and the ruler to score a line down the center of the noisemaker as shown on the pattern. Fold the noisemaker in half.

SAFETY TIP: *Make sure an adult helps you when using a knife.*

CHEERY GARLANDS

These jolly garlands will fill your room with party cheer. Because the paper is folded accordion-style into equal sections, any shape can be cut from it to make a string of repeating designs.

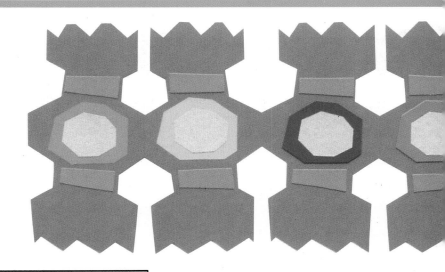

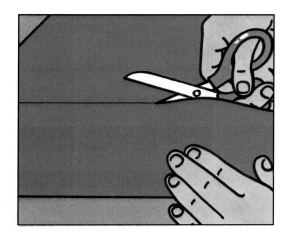

1 For the party favor garland, cut a strip of colored card stock 4 inches wide and as long as you like (long garlands can be made by taping small sections together). For the snowmen garland, cut a strip 6 1/4 inches wide.

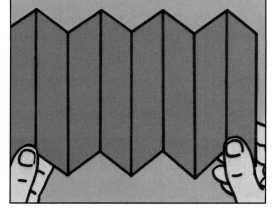

2 For the party favor garland, pleat the paper by folding it into 2-inch sections backward then forward to make an accordion fold. Try to keep the sections neat and even. For the snowmen garland, pleat the paper into 2 3/4-inch sections.

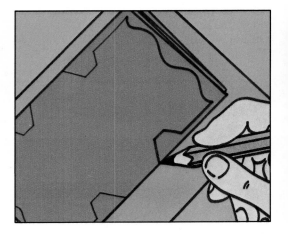

3 Using the pencil and tracing paper, trace the party favor or snowman pattern on page 87, and place the tracing facedown on your folded card stock. Trace over the lines to transfer the shape onto the card stock.

YOU WILL NEED

Colored card stock
Ruler
Pencil
Scissors
Tracing paper
Scraps of colored paper
All-purpose glue

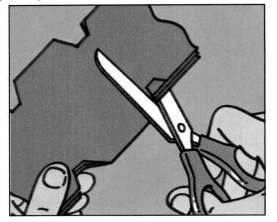

4 Cutting through all the layers at the same time, carefully cut around the shape you have drawn, making sure you leave some of the paper joined at the folds.

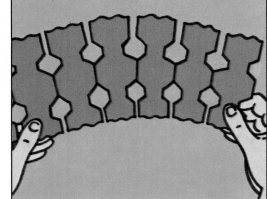

5 Carefully open the garland to see a string of your designs joined together.

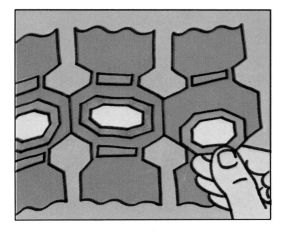

6 Cut small shapes from the colored paper, and glue them to your designs as decorations. Follow the pictures here to guide you.

FRUITY CARDS

Bright, colorful fruity shapes make wonderful novelty cards that can be used as party invitations, birthday cards, or even thank-you notes. Make the juicy pineapple or the succulent strawberry shown here, or design your own fruity shapes, following the steps to guide you.

1 Using the pencil and tracing paper, trace the main pineapple and strawberry patterns on page 88.

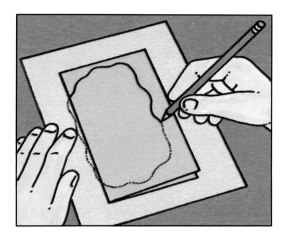

2 Fold a sheet of the yellow paper in half. Lay your pineapple tracing facedown on one side of the folded paper, making sure that one side of your pattern lies against the fold. Trace over the outline to transfer the shape onto the paper. Do the same for the strawberry tracing, transferring it onto a sheet of red paper.

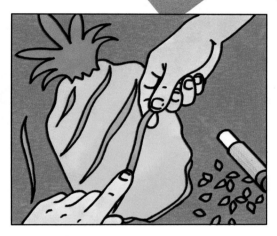

3 Cut out the folded shapes, leaving the side next to the fold still joined. Using the pencil and tracing paper, trace the stalk patterns on page 88. Lay the tracings facedown on green paper, and trace over the outlines to transfer the shapes onto the paper. Glue the stalks to the pineapple and strawberry as shown.

4 Cut wavy strips of orange paper, and glue these in crisscross patterns on the pineapple. Cut small green seed shapes, and glue these in between the orange strips. Cut small seed shapes from yellow paper, and glue them in a random pattern on the strawberry. Write your message inside the card.

YOU WILL NEED

Pencil
Tracing paper
Yellow, red, green, and
   orange paper
Scissors
Glue stick

BENDY ANIMALS

You can bend the pipe cleaner limbs of these cute creatures into lots of different funny positions. Hang them from picture frames, shelves, or the backs of chairs. They make fun decorations, which your guests can take home when the party is over.

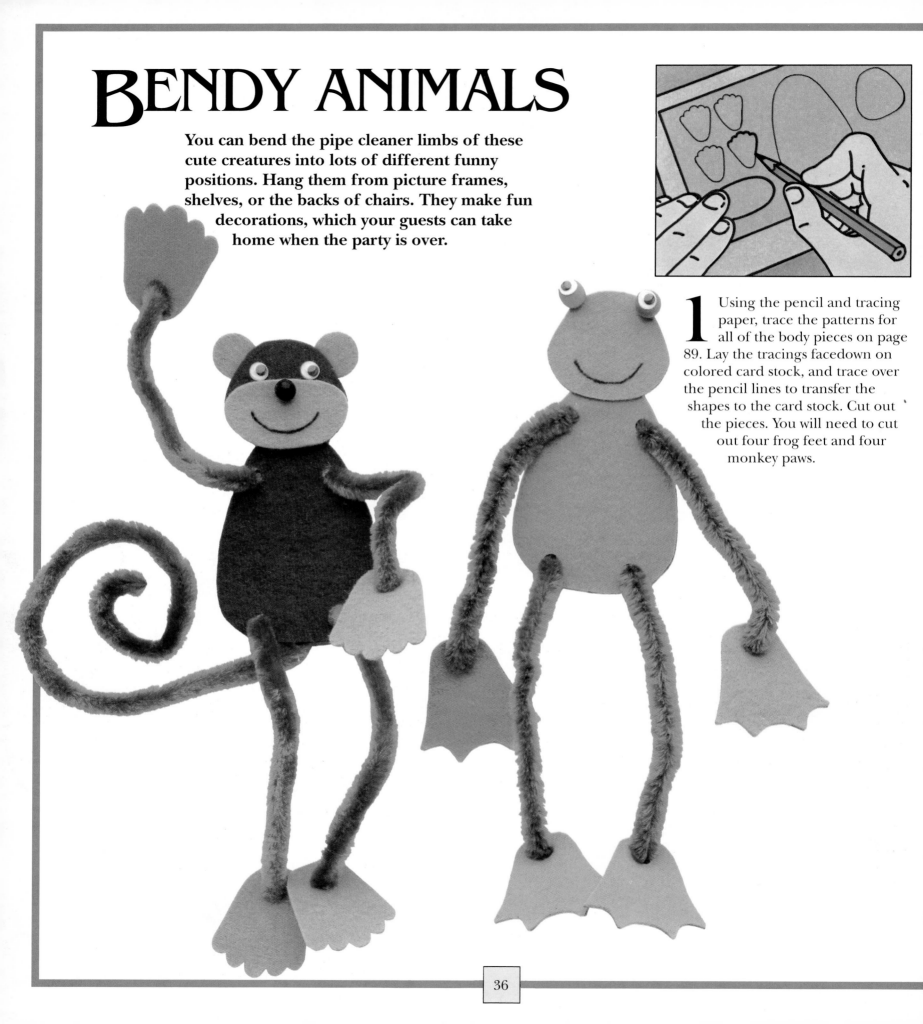

1 Using the pencil and tracing paper, trace the patterns for all of the body pieces on page 89. Lay the tracings facedown on colored card stock, and trace over the pencil lines to transfer the shapes to the card stock. Cut out the pieces. You will need to cut out four frog feet and four monkey paws.

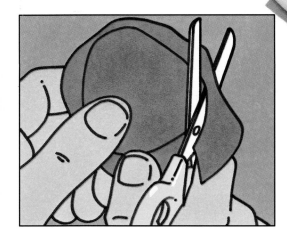

2 Using the compass, draw two circles with ³/₄-inch diameters on the brown card stock for the monkey's ears. Cut them out. Glue all the card pieces to colored felt — brown and tan for the monkey, green for the frog. Carefully cut around the edge of each piece of card stock to trim off any extra felt. Using a hole punch, make holes in the pieces as shown on the patterns.

3 Glue the monkey's muzzle to its head and the ears into position behind the head. Draw smiles on both faces using a black felt-tip pen. Glue the heads to the bodies.

4 Glue a black bead nose to the monkey's face, and glue two green beads for eye sockets onto the frog as shown. Glue joggle eyes onto each creature, using the pictures here to guide you. Cut two 5-inch lengths of pipe cleaner for the arms and two 6-inch lengths for the legs for each animal.

5 Insert the arms and legs through the holes in the feet and paws, and glue the ends to the undersides. Push the free ends of the pipe cleaners through the holes in each body, and glue the ends to the underside. Glue an extra pipe cleaner to the monkey as a tail.

YOU WILL NEED

Pencil; tracing paper
Brown, tan, and green card stock and scraps of felt
Scissors
Compass; hole punch
All-purpose glue
Black felt-tip pen
Black and green beads
Joggle eyes
Brown and green pipe cleaners

CLAY CHARACTER NAPKIN RINGS

These friendly-faced napkin rings can be easily adapted to make many different characters to suit any party theme. For added fun, you could even make ones that look like your party guests.

1 Roll a ball of clay about 1 inch in diameter for each face. Flatten it with the palm of your hand until the circle measures 1½ inches across. Roll a small ball of clay for the nose, and press it into the center of the face. Press the head of a pin into the clay to make eyes. To make the angel's eyes and mouth, draw slits using the pin point.

2 Ask an adult to help you bake the clay in the oven following the instructions on the package. When the clay is cool, glue coils of yellow yarn to the angel's head. Using a compass, draw a circle 1¼ inches in diameter on gold card stock, and cut it out. Glue it behind the angel's head.

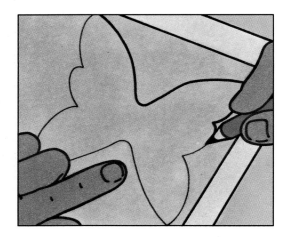

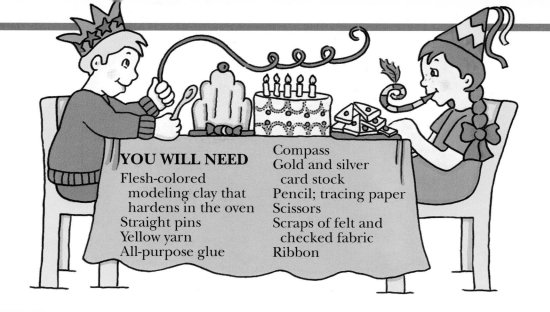

YOU WILL NEED

Flesh-colored
   modeling clay that
   hardens in the oven
Straight pins
Yellow yarn
All-purpose glue

Compass
Gold and silver
   card stock
Pencil; tracing paper
Scissors
Scraps of felt and
   checked fabric
Ribbon

3 Using the pencil and tracing paper, trace the pattern for the angel's wings on page 89. Lay the tracing facedown on the silver card stock, and trace over the lines to transfer the shape onto the card stock. Cut out the shape, and glue it to the back of the angel.

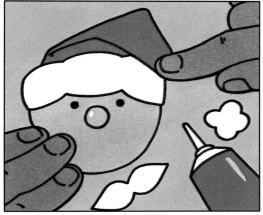

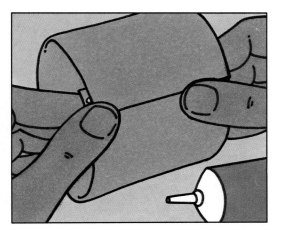

4 Using the pencil and tracing paper, trace the Santa and cowboy patterns on page 89. Cut out the tracing paper shapes, and pin them to the felt. Cut out the felt pieces, using the patterns to guide you. Unpin the tracing paper shapes. Glue the hats, beards, and moustaches in place as shown.

5 Glue a strip of ribbon around the cowboy hat. Cut out a 3-inch square of checked fabric. Fold it in half diagonally, and glue it under the cowboy's face. Cut a strip of felt measuring 5 inches by 1½ inches for each napkin ring. Overlap the ends, and glue them into place. Glue a face onto each napkin ring.

SAFETY TIP: *Make sure an adult helps you when using an oven.*

FIERY FIREWORKS

These star-spangled fireworks make the perfect goody boxes for a Fourth of July party or a party with a space age theme! They not only look the part, but they are just the right size for hiding a sweet treat or small gift inside.

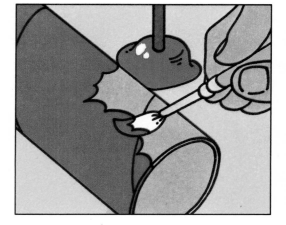

1 Paint the toilet paper tube and dowel with poster paints, and leave them to dry; the end of the dowel can be stuck into plastic clay to hold it while it dries.

4 Glue a dowel inside the tube. Wrap a gift in tissue paper, and slip it inside the tube. Scrunch up some more tissue paper, and push it into the open end of the tube to keep the gift safe inside.

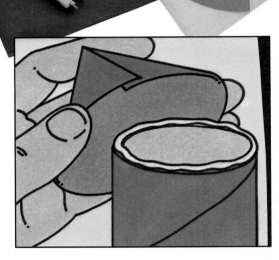

3 Dab glue on the rim of one end of the toilet paper tube, and press the cone onto the glue. Decorate the tube with star stickers.

2 To make the cone for the top of the rocket, use a compass to draw a circle with a 4-inch diameter on the colored paper. Cut it out, and cut a slit from the edge of the circle to the center. Cut out a slice measuring roughly one third of the circle, and then overlap the cut edges. Glue them into place.

YOU WILL NEED

Toilet paper tube	Thick colored paper
$1/4$-inch dowel	Scissors; ruler
Poster paints	All-purpose glue
Paintbrush	Star stickers
Plastic clay	Small gifts
Compass; pencil	Tissue paper

ANIMAL GIFT TAGS

Add the perfect finishing touch to your presents with these friendly animal gift tags. They are quick and simple to make and look fantastic. Choose from the cute black cat, the wriggling caterpillar, or the sweet ladybug or bee. Or simply cut out motifs from animal-patterned wrapping paper, like the frog shown here.

2 Cut two strips of sticky-backed velour ½ inch wide for the bumble bee, and stick them across the yellow oval. Trim off any extra velour, and fold the oval in half lengthwise. Glue two beads to one end for eyes. Twist the middle of a candy wrapper, and glue it to the center of your bee as wings.

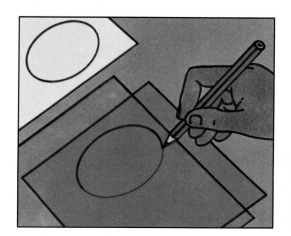

1 Using the pencil and tracing paper, trace the oval pattern on page 88. Lay the tracing facedown on the yellow card stock, and trace over the lines to transfer the shape onto the card stock. Transfer the shape onto red card stock in the same way, and cut out both ovals.

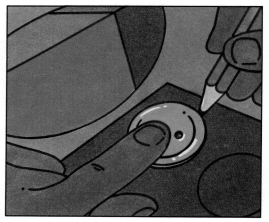

3 Cut a strip of sticky-backed velour ½ inch wide for the ladybug. Stick the strip over one end of the red oval, and trim it to the oval shape. Fold the oval in half lengthwise. Using a button, coin, or bottle top, draw two circles on the sticky-backed velour, and cut them out. Stick them to the ladybug's back. Glue two beads to the head for eyes.

4 To make the wriggling caterpillar, glue some scraps of wrapping paper onto card stock. Draw circles on the card stock about 1¼ inches wide, using a bottle top, coin, or button as a template. Cut them out, and glue the circles together, overlapping the edges. Glue two beads to one end for eyes.

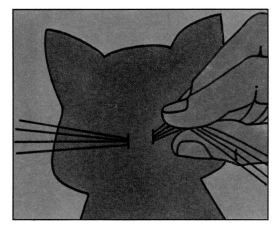

YOU WILL NEED
Pencil; tracing paper
Yellow, red, and black card stock
Scissors; ruler
Black sticky-backed velour
Small beads; all-purpose glue
Candy wrappers
Bottle top, button, or coin
Scraps of wrapping paper
White toy-making whiskers
Joggle eyes
Hole punch; narrow ribbon

5 Using the pencil and tracing paper, trace the cat pattern on page 89. Transfer the shape onto card stock following the instructions in step 1. Stick sticky-backed velour onto the back of the card stock. Cut out the shape you have drawn, and make holes as marked using a sharp pencil. Thread the white whiskers in and out of the holes in the center so they show on the velour side. Stick them in place with a dab of glue on the back. Glue the joggle eyes into position.

6 Roughly cut out a motif from a sheet of wrapping paper like the frog shown here. Glue it onto card stock, and cut out the picture neatly to make a quick and simple gift tag. Using a hole punch, punch a hole in each gift tag as shown, and thread narrow ribbon through each gift tag.

BALLOON ANIMALS

Balloon animals are always great fun, and they make exciting party decorations or prizes for party guests. You will need to buy special modeling balloons from a stationery store, toy store, or magic shop. Use a balloon pump, or ask an adult to help you blow up the balloons.

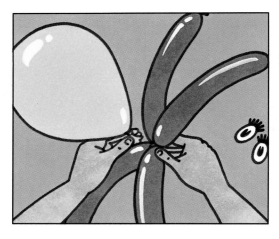

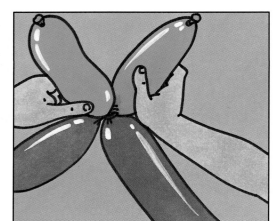

1 To make the octopus, blow up two short modeling balloons. Twist each balloon in the center, holding the twists in place with your fingers. Twist the two balloons together in the center to form an X. Blow up a round party balloon, and knot the end. Twist the knotted end around the twist in the modeling balloons. Stick on some eyes to decorate.

2 To make a dog, blow up one long and two short modeling balloons. Blow up a third short balloon halfway, so that it is very short. This will form the ears. Knot it, and cut off the extra piece of balloon. Twist the short balloon in half, and hold the twist in place while you twist a short section of the long balloon. Twist the two together to form the face and ears.

3 To form the neck, make another twist in the long balloon, creating a second section the same length as the face. Twist one of the short balloons in half, and twist it onto the twist in the long balloon to make the front legs. Make back legs in the same way, and attach them to the other end of the long balloon, leaving a small section of the long balloon as a tail. Stick some eyes onto the head.

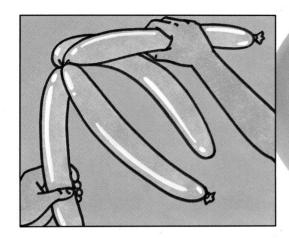

4 To make a swan, blow up two long modeling balloons. Twist them together to form an X as shown in step 1. Gather the four free ends into a bunch, which forms the tail, and twist them together so that they stay in place.

5 Blow up a third long balloon, pulling the balloon around in a curve as you blow. Leave some balloon uninflated at the end for the beak. Wind the mouth of the balloon around the center twist at the front of the body section. Stick on some eyes.

YOU WILL NEED

Balloon pump (optional)
Short modeling balloons
Ordinary round balloon
Stick-on eyes
Long modeling balloons
Scissors

CHRISTMAS WREATH

This starry wreath is easily made from salt dough and will delight and welcome your friends when it is hung on the door at Christmas. Paint it with bright colors, and add some glitter for a touch of Christmas sparkle.

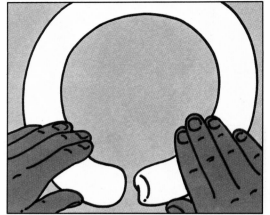

1 In the small bowl, mix the flour, salt, and water together to make a ball of dough. Roll a sausage of dough about 1¹/₄ inch thick, and bend it into a ring 8 inches in diameter. Cut off any extra dough, and put it to one side. Dampen the ends of the dough ring, and press them together.

2 Using the rolling pin, roll the remaining dough out flat until it is about ¹/₂ inch thick. Use the cookie cutter to cut out eleven stars. Gently place the boxes on the dough ring, making sure there are equal spaces between each box. Dampen the undersides of eight of the stars, and place them on the ring between the boxes.

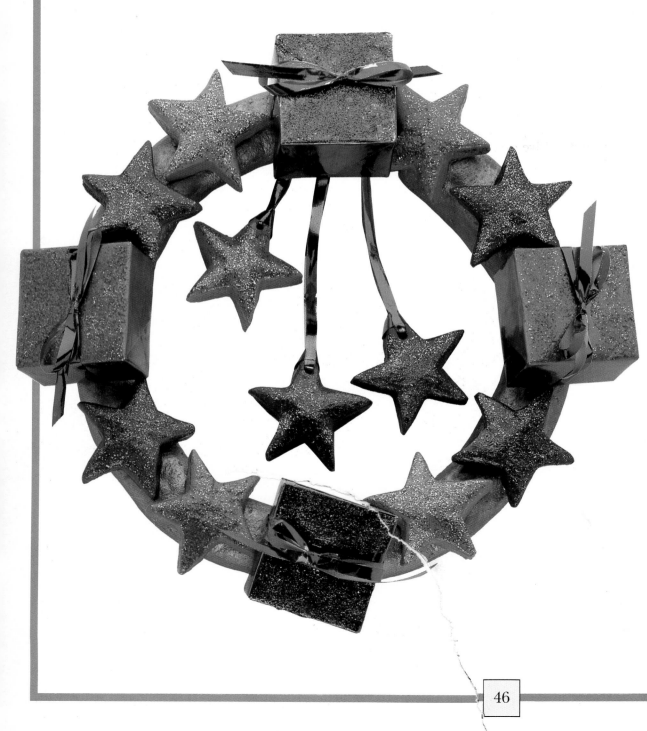

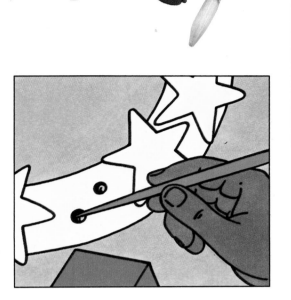

4 Ask an adult to help you bake the wreath and the extra stars in the oven for 8 hours at 250°F. When the wreath and stars have cooled, paint them with poster paints and leave them to dry. Give each piece five coats of varnish to seal it.

5 Thread a length of gift-wrapping ribbon through each extra star, forming a loop. Thread the ends of the ribbon loops through one pair of holes in the wreath. Hang the stars at different levels, knotting the ribbon ends on the back of the wreath. Thread a length of ribbon through each remaining pair of holes, replace the boxes, and tie the ribbons in tight bows to hold the boxes in place. Decorate the stars and boxes with glitter.

3 Gently remove the boxes. Use the knitting needle to pierce a pair of holes on the dough ring ¹/₄ inch apart where each box was. Pierce a hole through one point of each of the remaining three stars.

YOU WILL NEED
8 tablespoons plain flour
4 tablespoons salt
4 tablespoons water
Small bowl; rolling pin
Star-shaped cookie cutter
4 small wrapped boxes
Knitting needle
Poster paints and paintbrush
Craft varnish; glitter pens
Narrow gift-wrapping
　　　ribbon

SAFETY TIP: *Make sure an adult helps you when using an oven.*

MONSTER MASKS

Scary masks like these monster faces will be a treat at a spooky Halloween party. You could turn your mask making into a game by inviting your guests to make their own. Award a prize at the end of the party for the most terrifying monster mask.

YOU WILL NEED

Pencil; tracing paper
Colored card stock
Scissors
Craft knife (for adult use only)
All-purpose glue
Colored paper or shredded tissue paper
Brown felt-tip pen
Hat elastic
Colored stickers

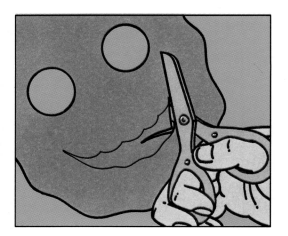

1 Using the pencil and tracing paper, trace the monster mask pattern on page 90. Place the tracing facedown on the the card stock, and trace over the outline, transferring the shape onto the card stock. Cut out the mask, and then cut out the holes for the mouth and eyes. Ask an adult to cut a slit for the nose using a craft knife.

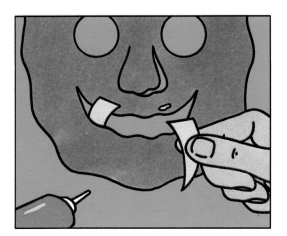

2 Cut out two tooth or fang shapes from cream or yellow card stock. Dab glue along the top edge of each tooth, and carefully stick them in place on the back of the mask just above the mouth hole.

3 Cut narrow strips of colored paper, and glue them upright behind the top of the mask, or scrunch up some shredded tissue paper and glue it to the front of the mask. If you want to add ears, follow the instructions in step 1 to transfer the pattern on page 90 onto card stock. Cut out the ears.

SAFETY TIP: *Make sure an adult helps you when using a craft knife.*

4 Draw details on the ears with a brown felt-tip pen, and glue them into position. Sharpen the pencil, and use it to pierce a hole on each side of the mask. Thread a length of hat elastic through the holes, knotting each end behind the holes. Decorate your mask with stickers.

49

SHINY MEDALS

Everybody loves to play party games, and if there are prizes for the winner, they're even more exciting. These sparkly medals look just the part but are even better than the real thing because they can be eaten. You can make gold, silver, and bronze medals for first, second, and third prize winners, or make a medal for each of your guests so that everyone can win.

1 Cut a length of ribbon long enough to fit over your head. Glue the ends together. You might like to leave one end longer than the other like the one shown here.

2 Decorate the foil-covered candies with stick-on stars and with shapes cut from foil candy wrappers. Use gold, silver, and bronze colors to make first, second, and third prize medals.

3 Using strong, all-purpose glue, stick the decorated candy along the bottom half of the ribbon with equal spaces in between.

4 Stick gold stars onto the ribbon in between the candies to make the medals extra sparkly.

YOU WILL NEED

Gold ribbon, 1 inch wide
Scissors
All-purpose glue
Foil-covered candies
Stick-on foil stars

BIRTHDAY CAKE CARDS

These attractive 3-D birthday cake cards, complete with candles and icing, make ideal greeting cards to send to friends. Or make some as invitations to your own birthday party.

YOU WILL NEED
Pencil; tracing paper
Colored and white card stock
Scissors; colored markers; ruler
14-inch lengths of 1-inch-
  wide ribbon
All-purpose glue

1 Using the pencil and tracing paper, trace the cake and icing patterns on page 91. Lay the tracing facedown on the colored card stock, and trace over the outline of the cake pattern to transfer it onto the card. Cut out the shape you have drawn.

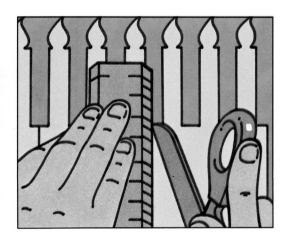

2 Transfer the icing shapes onto the white card stock following the instructions in step 1. Cut out both pieces. Use a marker to make a colored border along the edges of the icing pieces as shown. Using a scissor blade and the ruler, score both the icing sections and the main cake section along the dotted lines shown on the pattern.

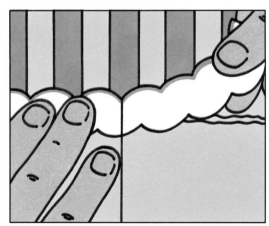

3 Apply a line of glue along the back of the icing sections. Glue the icing to the cake, taking care to line up the score lines as you go.

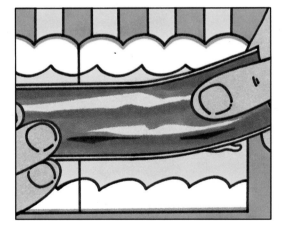

4 Glue the ribbons across the center of the cake. Turn the card over, and glue the ribbon ends to the back of the card to make a neat finish. Fold the card along the score lines to make a box shape.

SEASIDE CUPS AND STRAWS

These pretty seaside cups and straws are perfect for summer parties and bring a ray of sunshine to indoor beach parties in winter. Pretty shells can be collected next time you visit the beach, or draw pictures of shells and starfish onto card stock instead of the real thing.

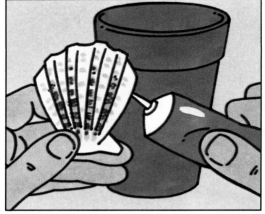

1 Make sure that your plastic cups and shells are clean and dry. Glue the shells and starfish to the cups. You can use tape to hold them in place until they are dry.

YOU WILL NEED
Plastic cups
Shells and starfish
Glue; scissors
Pencil; tracing paper
Colored card stock
Blue sticky-backed plastic
Sequins; yellow yarn
Felt-tip pens
Hole punch; cord
Round stickers
Cotton balls
Sticky foam pads
Drinking straws

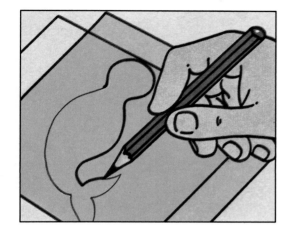

2 Using the pencil and tracing paper, trace the patterns for the mermaid, anchor, and ship on page 92. Lay the tracings facedown on colored card stock, and trace over the outlines to transfer the shapes onto the card stock. Cut out the shapes you have drawn.

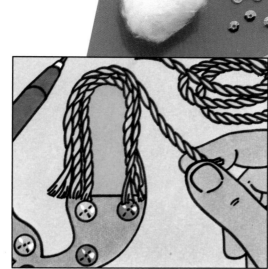

3 Stick blue sticky-backed plastic onto the lower half of the mermaid, and cut away any extra, using the edge of the card to guide you. Glue on some sequins as scales. Cut some short lengths of yellow yarn for hair, and glue it onto the head. Draw on the mermaid's face with black and red felt-tip pens.

4 Make a hole near the top of the anchor using the hole punch. Tie a short length of cord through the hole, and wrap it around the anchor, gluing it in place as you go. Dab the cut ends with glue to stop them from fraying.

5 Glue the two ship sections together as shown. Stick two small stickers in place for portholes. Glue a small tuft of cotton behind the funnel to finish. Use double-sided sticky-backed foam pads to attach your designs to drinking straws.

PRETTY PARTY PLATES

Party food always looks exciting and colorful, but it's even more fun to serve party food to your guests on these cheerful decorated plates. Colored paper can be cut to any shape or design to add a special finishing touch to simple paper plates. Make lots of different designs or a whole matching set, complete with knives and forks.

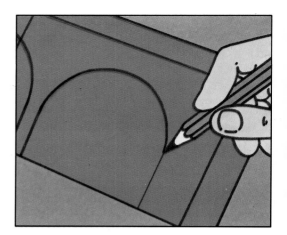

1 Using the pencil and tracing paper, trace the sun or petal shapes from page 92. Lay the tracings facedown on orange or pink card stock, tracing over the outlines to transfer the designs.

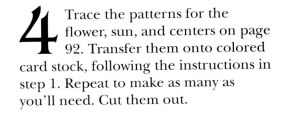

4 Trace the patterns for the flower, sun, and centers on page 92. Transfer them onto colored card stock, following the instructions in step 1. Repeat to make as many as you'll need. Cut them out.

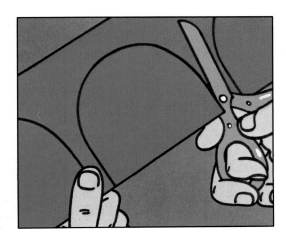

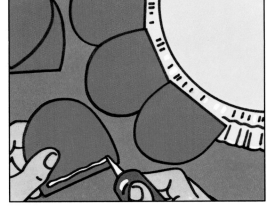

2 Repeat the process in step 1 to make as many flame or petal pieces as you need to fit around a plate. Cut them out.

3 Glue the paper pieces to the underside of the plate, overlapping them slightly, as shown here.

5 Glue the round center pieces into position on each sun and flower. Glue the suns and flowers halfway up the plastic cutlery, or wherever fits your hand comfortably. Cut a small oval shape for the bee, and decorate it with shapes cut from colored paper. Follow the photograph here to guide you. Glue the bee to a flower petal. You can glue on other decorations as well, such as the candy bee shown in the photograph.

PLACE CARDS

These amusing place cards will show your guests where to sit for a meal or for party treats. The clowns and dogs here suit most occasions, but it is also easy to adapt the designs to suit your own party theme. And when the celebrations are over, your guests can take their place cards home to remind them of the wonderful time they had.

1 For each place card, cut out one section from an egg carton. Glue a cotton-pulp ball on top for the head, and let it dry. Paint the model to look like a clown or a dog. When the paint has dried, use a felt-tip pen to draw on the face.

2 To make a crown for the clown, cut a strip of crepe paper with one zigzag edge. Glue the strip around the head, overlapping the ends. To make curly hair, pull gift-wrapping ribbon over a scissor blade to coil it. Glue pieces of ribbon to each side of the head.

3 Stand the clown on the colored card stock, and draw around the base of the egg carton. Draw two feet at the front, and cut out the card shape you have drawn. Spread glue around the base of the clown, and stick it to the feet. Decorate your clown with pompoms.

4 Pierce a hole on each side of the dog's head using a toothpick. Cut two short lengths of pipe cleaner, and push them into the holes to make ears, as shown. Pierce a hole in the lower edge of the dog's body for the tail. Cut a 2¹/₂-inch length of pipe cleaner, and push it into the hole.

YOU WILL NEED
Cardboard egg carton
Scissors; all-purpose glue
1¹/₄-inch cotton-pulp
balls (from craft shop)
Paints and paintbrush
Felt-tip pens
Crepe paper
Gift-wrapping
ribbon
Colored paper and card
stock
Pencil; pompoms
Plastic toothpicks
Thick pipe cleaners
Small beads

5 Cut strips of paper 1 inch wide, and write your guests' names on them. Glue one end of each strip around a toothpick to make a flag. To attach a flag to the clown, glue the toothpick into a bead, and glue the bead to the clown as a hand. Glue a second bead to the other side to make the other hand. Attach a flag to the dog by wrapping the dog's tail around the toothpick.

ANGEL PARTY PIÑATA

In Mexico, piñatas are traditional party decorations. Made from pottery and filled with candy and small gifts, they are hung up at parties, fiestas, and celebrations. Children hit the pot with sticks until it bursts and releases its hidden treasures. This angel piñata's sack is made from tissue paper, which makes it very easy to break.

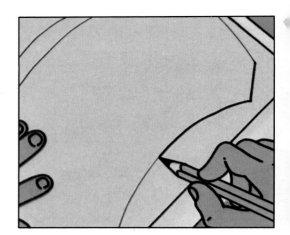

1 Using the pencil and tracing paper, trace the angel piñata main body pattern on page 93. Lay the pattern facedown on the thick pink card stock. Trace over the outlines to transfer the shape onto the card stock. Cut it out.

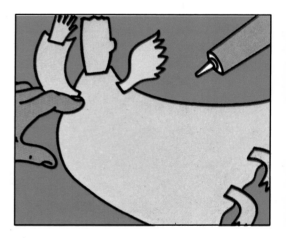

2 Follow the process in step 1 to cut the head, wing, halo, two arms, two hands, and two feet from suitably colored card stock. Glue all of these except the front arm and hand into place on the back of the angel as shown. Glue the hand to the front arm.

4 Using a scissor blade and the ruler, carefully score a line across the angel's front arm as shown on the pattern. Apply some glue to the top section of the arm, and glue just the top to the angel as shown.

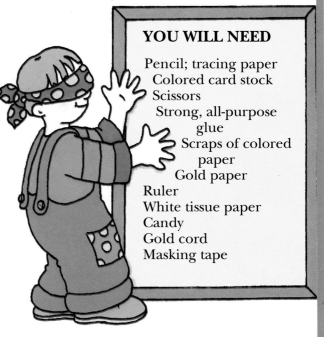

YOU WILL NEED

Pencil; tracing paper
Colored card stock
Scissors
Strong, all-purpose
glue
Scraps of colored
paper
Gold paper
Ruler
White tissue paper
Candy
Gold cord
Masking tape

3 Cut out a nose, mouth, and two eyes from scraps of colored paper, and glue these into place. Cut out some pleats and decorations from white and gold paper, and glue them on as well.

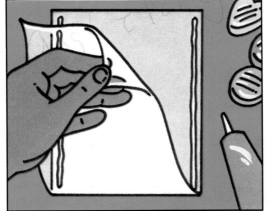

5 Cut a large rectangle of tissue paper, measuring about 16 1/2 inches long by 7 inches wide. Fold it in half, and glue along both long sides to make a bag. When the glue is dry, fill the bag with candy and tie the top closed with gold cord.

6 Cut a loop of cord, and attach it to the angel's back using masking tape or strong glue to form a hanger. Glue the bag of candy to the front of the angel, flapping its front arm over the top. Allow the glue to dry before hanging up your piñata.

ROCKET FOOD DISPENSER

No space age party would be complete without a shimmering rocket centerpiece for the party table. It is easily made from things you can find around the home and decorated with shapes cut from saved candy wrappers. This one is filled with candy, but you could fill it with chips, snacks, sandwiches, or any other party food.

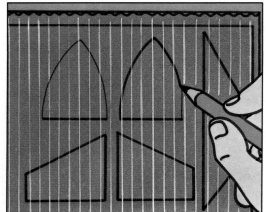

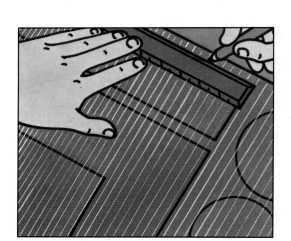

1 Using the pencil and ruler and following the templates and measurements on page 94, draw the rocket body and base patterns on corrugated cardboard. Make sure that the ridges of the cardboard run from the top to the bottom of the shapes. Use the compass to draw the two base circles, as shown on page 94. Cut out the shapes you have drawn.

2 Using the pencil and tracing paper, trace the fin patterns on page 94. Lay the tracings facedown on the corrugated cardboard, and trace over the outlines to transfer the shapes onto the cardboard. You will need to draw two of each shape. Cut them out.

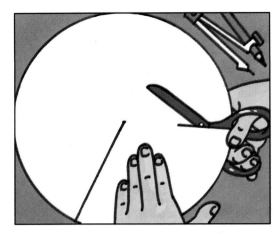

3 Using the compass, draw a circle on the thin card stock measuring 10½ inches in diameter. Cut out the circle, then cut out a one-third slice of it as shown. Fold the shape around to form a cone, and glue or tape the edges together.

4 Use the blade of the scissors to lightly score down the ridges of the cardboard of the main body and base. Gently bend the cardboard to form two tubes, and tape the ends in place. Tape the large base circle from step 1 on top of the base. Tape the small fins to the main body. Tape the large fin sections together, then tape them to the rocket base. Glue the main body of the rocket to the base.

5 Use the scissors to snip off the very tip of the nose cone. Glue the nose cone to the top of the rocket. Glue the wooden bead to the end of a small section of drinking straw, and push the other end of the straw into the top of the cone to form an antenna. Cut the foil into manageable pieces, and glue it to cover the entire rocket.

YOU WILL NEED
Pencil; ruler
Corrugated cardboard
Compass; scissors
Tracing paper
All-purpose glue
Masking tape
Thin card stock
Small wooden bead
Drinking straw
Aluminum foil
Foil candy wrappers
Stick-on gold stars
Tinsel
Small bowl of candy

6 Cut decorations from candy wrappers, and glue them on the rocket. Add stick-on stars for a sparkly effect. Glue or tape the tinsel inside the rocket, just above the main opening, and trim it to the correct length. Take the small base circle from step 1, cover it with aluminum foil, and glue it to the base to form a stand for the bowl. Place the small bowl, filled with candy or other snacks, inside the rocket.

EXOTIC BOTTLE BIRDS

These chirpy feathered friends provide the perfect disguise for bottles of soda or juice and are sure to amuse your guests. By using different size bottles, you can make a fun family of birds like the one shown here.

1 Using the pencil and tracing paper, trace the large or small beak pattern (depending on the size of your bottle) on page 95. Lay the tracing facedown on the card stock. Trace over the outline to transfer the shape onto the card stock. Cut out the beak, and use a scissor blade and the ruler to score the beak along the dotted lines.

YOU WILL NEED:

Pencil; tracing paper
Yellow and orange card stock
Scissors; ruler
Bottles of soda or fruit juice
All-purpose glue
Joggle eyes
Colored feathers
Black felt-tip pen

2 Fold the beak in half along the scored line, and fold the tabs under. Glue the tabs to the neck of the bottle. Glue a pair of joggle eyes onto the bottle just above the beak.

3 Glue colored feathers to the sides of the bottle for wings. Bunch together a group of feathers, and glue them to the top of the bottle as a crest. Using a felt-tip pen, draw nostrils onto the beak.

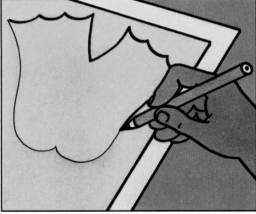

4 To make the feet, stand your bottle on the feet patterns on page 95, and choose the size that best suits your bottle. Transfer the pattern onto the card stock, following the instructions in step 1. Cut out the feet, and glue them to the bottle base.

SWEET CREATURES

These cute creatures are made of the type of clay that hardens in the oven and can be wrapped around sticks of candy, lollipops, or other sweets to give to your guests as gifts.

1 To make the crocodile, roll out the green clay until it's 1/4 inch thick. Using the pencil and tracing paper, trace the pattern on page 95. Lay the tracing facedown on card stock, and trace over the outline to transfer the shape onto the card stock. Cut the shape out. Lay the card template on the clay, and cut around it using a blunt knife.

YOU WILL NEED
Colored clay that hardens in the oven
Rolling pin
Pencil; tracing paper
Card stock; scissors
Blunt knife or modeling tool
Straight pin
Aluminum foil
Lollipops, sticks of candy, and other sweets
Clear, nontoxic varnish
Joggle eyes (optional)
Feathers; all-purpose glue

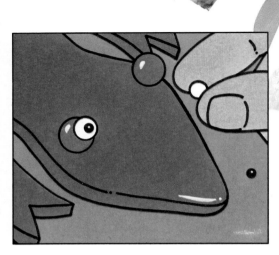

2 Smooth the cut edges of the clay. Roll two small balls of green clay for the eye sockets, and place them on the head. To make the eyes, add two small balls of white clay, then two smaller balls of black. Using the pin, draw a crisscross pattern on the croc's back and a mouth on its face.

4 Use white and black clay to make the seal's eyes. (Or if you prefer, you can glue on joggle eyes after the seal has been baked and varnished.) Press together a small ball of green clay and a small ball of blue clay, and roll them together to make one ball. Press this to the front of your seal.

3 To make the basking seal, roll a sausage of black clay about 2³⁄₄ inches long and ³⁄₄ inches thick. Bend the sausage, and squeeze each end to a point. Roll out some black clay until it is ¹⁄₄ inch thick. Follow the method in step 1 to cut out a tail and two fins using the patterns on page 95. Press these onto the body.

SAFETY TIP: *Make sure an adult helps you when using an oven.*

5 To make a bird, roll a ball of blue clay about 1¹⁄₂ inches wide for the body, and stretch it into an oval. Roll another ball 1 inch wide for the head, and press it onto the body. Roll out some blue clay and some orange or yellow clay, and follow the instructions in step 1 to cut out the wings, feet, and a beak using the patterns on page 95. Press these onto the bird as shown.

6 Roll two small balls of black clay, and press them to the bird's head as eyes. Pierce a hole in the back of the bird for the tail. Mold some aluminum foil into the shape of your candies. Wrap a creature around each foil mold, and ask an adult to bake them all in the oven following the instructions on the clay package. Leave the creatures to cool, and then varnish them. Glue small feathers into the hole in the bird to make a tail.

HAPPY-FACE CAKE

This smiling-faced clown cake is easy to make and will be the cheerful highlight of any party. Decorate it with bright candies and cake decorations, and finish with a bright crepe-paper bow tie.

1 Place the cherry just below the center of the cake to make a nose. Arrange candied orange slices in the shape of a big smiling mouth, using the pictures here to guide you. Add a small pink mint at each end of the mouth for cheeks.

2 Arrange six jelly diamonds in a star shape for each eye, and place a small yellow mint in the center. Press a silver nonpareil into the center of each jelly diamond. Place a lemon jelly slice above each eye to make eyebrows.

68

YOU WILL NEED

Cake with white frosting
Cherry
Candied orange and
lemon slices
2 small pink mints
Candy jelly
diamonds
2 small yellow mints
Silver nonpareils
Candied licorice bits
Multicolored sprinkles
Crepe paper; scissors
All-purpose glue; clear tape
Colored stickers
Toothpick

5 Cut a 1-inch-wide strip of crepe paper, and wrap this around the center of the bow tie to cover the tape. Decorate the bow tie with bright-colored stickers.

3 Scatter candy-covered licorice bits around the top edge of the cake to make the hair. Place multicolored sprinkles around the clown's eyes.

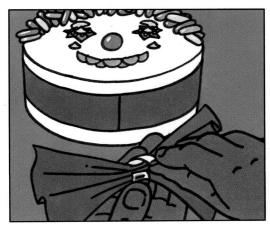

4 Cut a strip of crepe paper, and wrap it around the side of the cake. Overlap the ends, and glue them together. Cut an 8-inch square of crepe paper for the bow tie. Bunch up the middle, and hold it in position with clear tape.

6 To attach the bow tie to the cake, push a toothpick halfway down into the front side of the cake. Carefully push the bow tie onto the toothpick. Remember to remove the bow tie and toothpick before the cake is cut.

FUN-FILLED SANDWICHES

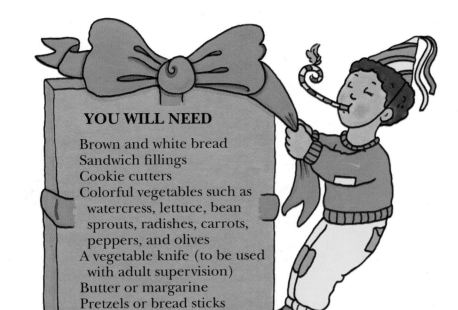

YOU WILL NEED

Brown and white bread
Sandwich fillings
Cookie cutters
Colorful vegetables such as watercress, lettuce, bean sprouts, radishes, carrots, peppers, and olives
A vegetable knife (to be used with adult supervision)
Butter or margarine
Pretzels or bread sticks
Plates

Sandwiches are a traditional party food. You can make them extra special by cutting them into interesting shapes and decorating them with fresh vegetables. Ask an adult to help you slice up some colorful vegetables before you start, and then you can let your imagination run wild, transforming your sandwiches into exciting animals in their own lettuce landscapes.

SAFETY TIP: *Make sure an adult helps you when using a sharp knife.*

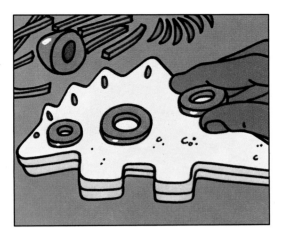

1 Make some sandwiches using the bread and fillings of your choice. Do not overfill them, because they are easier to cut when they are flat.

2 Carefully stamp out different shapes using cookie cutters. Keep any leftover bread to feed to the birds.

3 Ask an adult to help you cut some colorful vegetables into small pieces. Use a little butter or margarine to stick the pieces on top of the sandwich shapes as decoration. Add pretzels or bread sticks as well.

4 Make a landscape on each serving plate using bean sprouts for grass, watercress or lettuce for trees, as well as grated carrot and any other suitable vegetables. Place your sandwiches in the landscape, and serve.

JELL-O POTS

These pretty flowerpots look so sweet and make a real change to the usual cake or ice cream. The flowers are lollipops trimmed with crepe paper, and the pots are old yogurt containers filled with fruit and Jell-O.

1 Make sure the yogurt containers are clean and dry before you start. Paint the containers in bright colors, and leave them to dry. Decorate by painting on hearts and flowers in contrasting colors.

2 Fill the containers with fruit. Ask an adult to help you make the Jell-O following the instructions on the package. Pour it over the fruit, and leave the containers in the refrigerator until the Jell-O has set.

3 Cut a strip of crepe paper 9¹/₂ inches long by 1¹/₂ inches wide. Cut six petal shapes along one edge. Scrunch up the long, straight edge, and glue it behind a lollipop. Repeat to make a flower for each container.

4 Just before you are ready to eat, push the end of a flower lollipop into each of the containers of Jell-O, and serve immediately.

SAFETY TIP: *Make sure an adult helps you when handling hot liquids.*

CREEPY-CRAWLIES

The perfect sweet treat for Halloween parties, these easy-to-make creepy spiders may look scary, but they taste delicious. Any small chocolate cakes can be used for the bodies, and the legs are thick strings of licorice.

YOU WILL NEED

Chocolate cookies or cupcakes
Small candies
Thick strands of licorice
Scissors

74

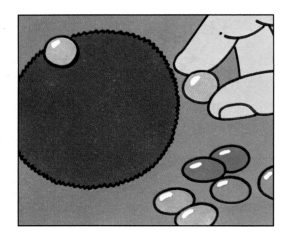

1 Press two small round candies into the top of each cookie or cupcake to make the spider's eyes.

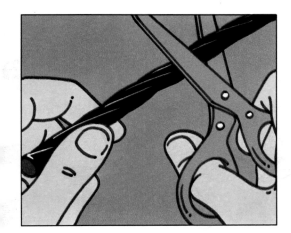

2 Using the scissors, cut the licorice strings into eight equal lengths to make the legs. Use the thickest licorice for the best effect and to be sure that the legs can support the weight of the cake body.

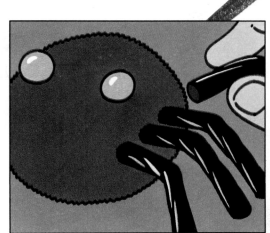

3 Bend the legs to get a curved shape. You may have to bend them right in half to make the curved shape hold when you release them. Press four legs into each side of each cake.

4 Press on candies for the mouth. Use different shaped candies to make spiders that look happy, sad, friendly, or fierce.

WITCH'S BREW

This special spooky brew is an ideal drink for a Halloween party. A goldfish bowl makes the perfect cauldron, and the fire is built from pretzels or chocolate-covered cookies.

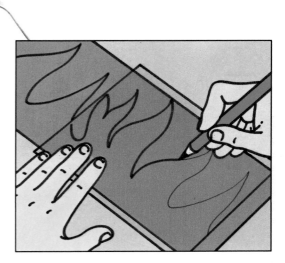

1 Cut a long strip of thin red paper. Using a pencil, draw two or three flame shapes onto tracing paper. Lay the tracing facedown on the red paper, and trace over the lines to transfer the shape onto the paper. Move the tracing along, and trace over the lines again, repeating the process until the pattern runs the whole length of the red paper. Cut the pattern out to make a long strip of flames.

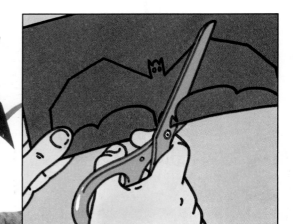

2 Using the pencil and tracing paper, trace the bat pattern from page 95. Lay the tracing facedown on the black paper, and trace over the lines to transfer the shape. Cut out two or more bats to decorate the bowl. Punch out eyes using a sharp pencil point.

3 Fill the bowl with limeade. If you don't have limeade, you can color lemonade with a few drops of green food coloring.

4 Pull the paper flames around the base of the bowl, overlapping the ends. Tape the ends in place, and cut off any extra paper. Tape the bats onto the bowl.

5 Build a fire around the bowl using pretzels or chocolate-covered cookies. Add a few jelly snakes creeping around the fire and a ladle to serve the brew.

YOU WILL NEED

Red paper
Scissors
Pencil; tracing paper
Black paper
Clean, round glass bowl
Limeade
Clear tape
Pretzels or chocolate-
    covered cookies
Jelly snakes
Ladle

JAZZY JUICERS

These exotic drinks are simple to make and add a splash of color to any party table. They suit any occasion but are great for summer or beach parties. Choose from the desert island Blue Lagoon or the fruity Sunburst.

1 To make the sunburst drink, pour a little raspberry syrup into the bottom of a glass. Gently fill the rest of the glass with orange juice so that the two drinks mix only in the middle to give a sunrise effect.

YOU WILL NEED
Glasses (if possible, ones with built-in twirling straws, as shown)
Drinking straws (if needed)
Thick raspberry syrup
Orange juice
Fruit slices
Pencil; scissors
Green card stock
Chocolate sticks
Fondant icing
Blue food coloring
Lemonade; ice cream

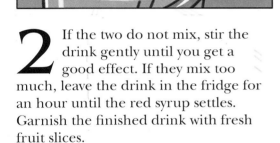

2 If the two do not mix, stir the drink gently until you get a good effect. If they mix too much, leave the drink in the fridge for an hour until the red syrup settles. Garnish the finished drink with fresh fruit slices.

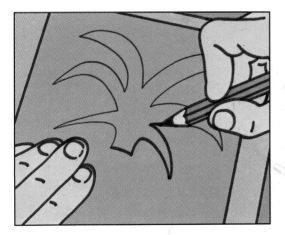

3 To make the twirlers for the blue lagoon drink, draw a palm-tree top on green card stock using the picture here to guide you. Cut this shape out, and repeat this step to make two twirlers for each drink.

4 Stick one treetop to the top of a chocolate stick with a little fondant icing. If you don't have icing, sticky jam will work just as well.

5 Pour a couple of drops of blue food coloring into a glass. Fill the glass with lemonade, and stir to give an even color.

6 Add a scoop of ice cream to the top of the drink to make an island, and push two palm tree twirlers into the island. Serve immediately.

GAMES TO PLAY

No party would be complete without fun games for you and your guests to play. You can award small gifts as prizes to the winners, and in some games, everybody wins.

MUSICAL CUSHIONS

For this fun party game, you will need a cassette player or radio, and a cushion or pillow for each person playing.

1 Scatter the cushions on the floor around the room. While the music plays, the players walk or dance around the room.

2 When the music stops, each player must sit on a cushion with no part of their body touching the floor.

3 At the start of each round, one of the cushions is removed. The player who can't find a cushion to sit on when the music stops is out. The last player left wins the game.

ANIMAL ANTICS

You will need an even number of players for this game. Before you start, write down some animal names on small slips of paper. You should write the same name on two slips of paper to make matching pairs. Make enough slips so that there is one for each guest.

1 Fold all the pieces of paper in half, and mix them around in a box, bowl, or hat.

2 Players take a slip of paper and walk around the room making the noise of the animal written on it until they find the other player making the same noise. Everyone wins a prize in this game.

ORANGE CHINS

This game doesn't need much preparation. All you will need is a couple of oranges and some friends to play it with.

1 Divide the players into two teams and ask them to stand in two rows.

2 Give the first player in each row an orange, which he or she tucks under his or her chin.

3 On the starter's orders, the team must pass the orange down the row from chin to chin without using their hands. If the orange is dropped, it should be picked up and the passing should continue.

4 The first team to get their orange to the end is the winner.

WITCH'S FOOTSTEPS

Choose one player to be the witch. The witch stands with his or her back to the other players with a prize by his or her side.

1 The players must creep up on the witch while his or her back is turned. When the witch turns around to look (which the witch can do as often as he or she pleases), the players must freeze and stand as still as statues.

2 If the witch spots the slightest movement, he or she points to the player and that person is out. The winner is the first person to reach the prize without being caught by the witch.

BALLOON RACE
This game is lots of fun, but you have to be careful not to pop the balloons as you play.

1 Set start and finish points for the race, which will be run with a balloon between each player's knees.

2 On the starter's orders, the players must race to the finish, keeping the balloon between their knees. Any player who drops his or her balloon must return to the start.

FLOATING FEATHERS
This is an ideal game if there isn't much room to play in. Have all of the players sit in a small circle and stay seated.

1 A feather is dropped into the center of the circle, and the players must blow or flap their hands to keep the feather up in the air.

2 If the feather touches anyone, he or she is out of the game. The winner is the last player left in.

EASTER EGG HUNT
Prepare for this game by hiding lots of small chocolate eggs all over the house.

1 Give each guest a basket or bag, and send them all off around the house to collect as many eggs as they can find.

2 This Easter game can be played at any time of the year by replacing the eggs with other small gifts or candies that suit your party theme.

FUNNY FACES
This activity is great fun for everyone and provides a personal souvenir for each party guest.

1 Ask an adult to help you paint a funny body on a large sheet of stiff card. Check that the height is right (see step 2) before cutting out a hole where the face should be.

2 Lean the card upright against the back of a chair, and invite guests to kneel on the chair and put their faces through the hole.

3 Take a photograph of each person; instant cameras are best, since the guests can take their pictures home with them. Photographs that have to be developed can be sent out to each guest a few days after the party as a thank-you note and souvenir in one.

PATTERNS

The following pages show the patterns and templates you will need to make many of the projects in this book. To find out how to copy a pattern, follow the step-by-step instructions given for each project. In most cases, a tracing of one of the patterns here can be transferred straight onto the paper or card stock you are using to make the project. These patterns can also be used to make cardboard templates. These are ideal for making lots of the same shape, transferring patterns to materials such as clay, or making permanent patterns that can be kept in a safe place and used time and time again.

**BEAUTIFUL
BUTTERFLY MASKS**
Page **10**

Butterfly Mask

Cut out.

Cut out.

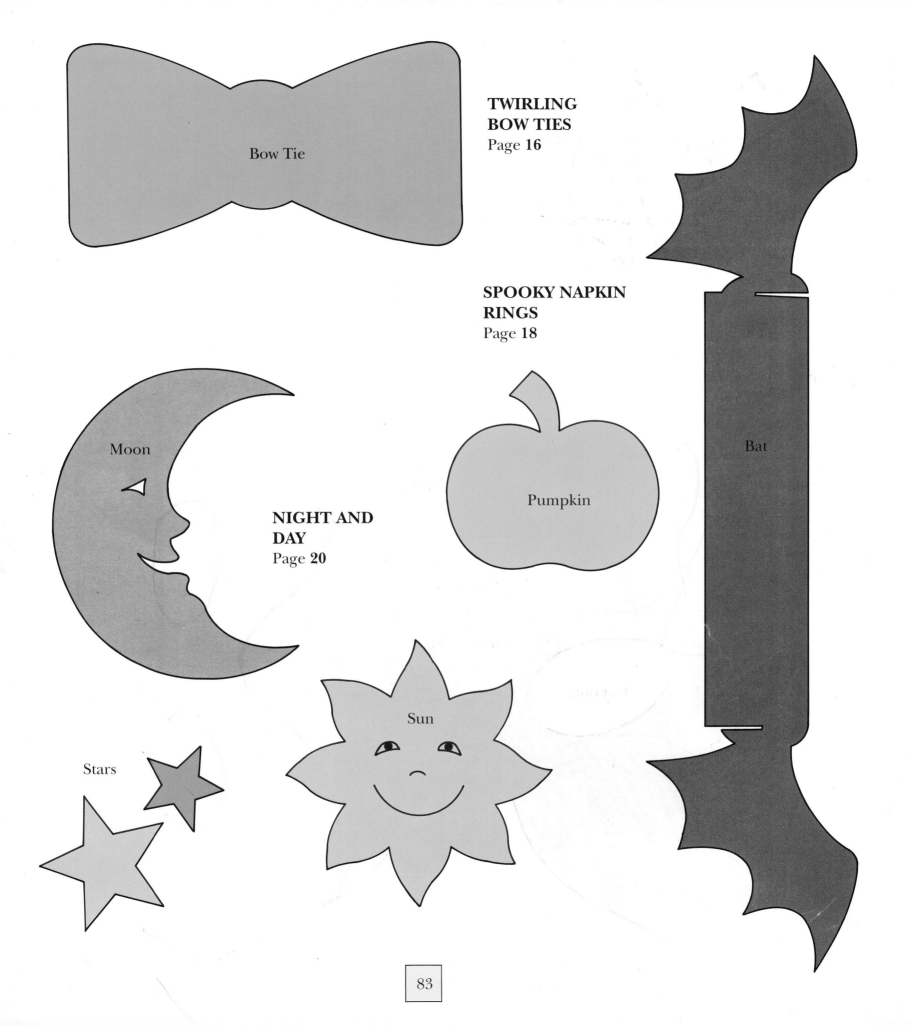

Bow Tie

**TWIRLING
BOW TIES**
Page **16**

**SPOOKY NAPKIN
RINGS**
Page **18**

Moon

**NIGHT AND
DAY**
Page **20**

Pumpkin

Bat

Stars

Sun

83

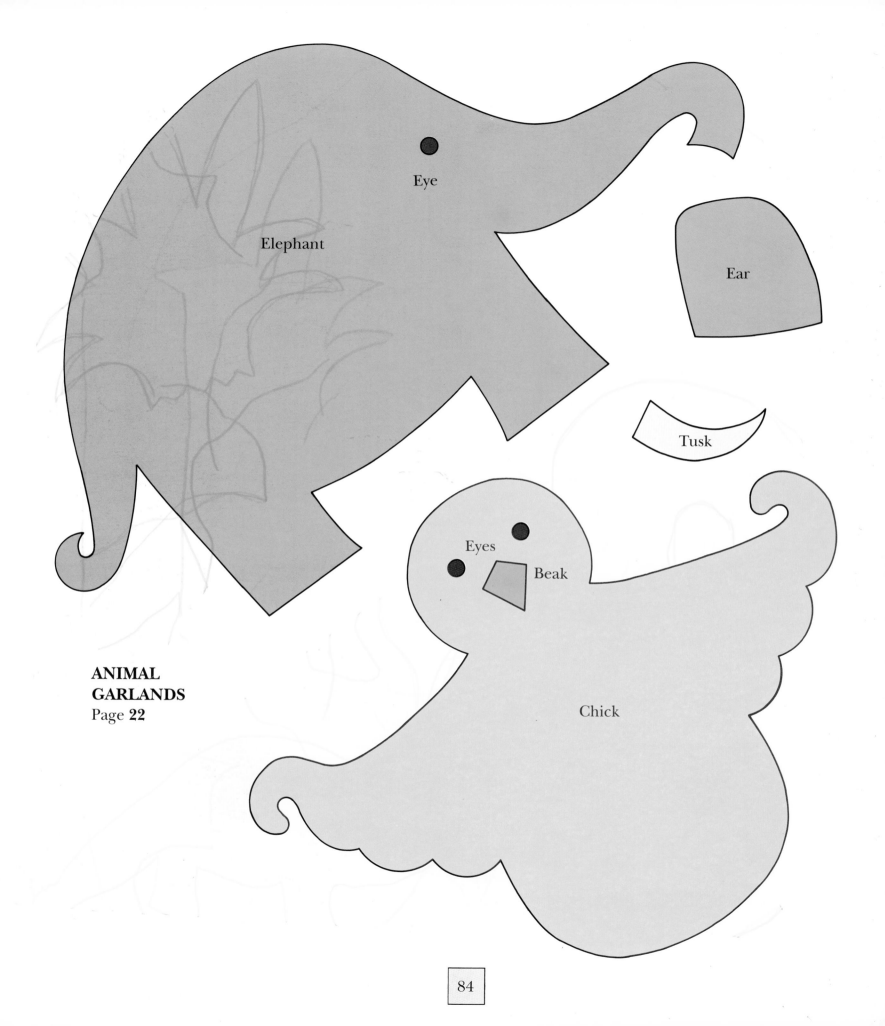

Eye

Elephant

Ear

Tusk

Eyes

Beak

Chick

**ANIMAL
GARLANDS**
Page **22**

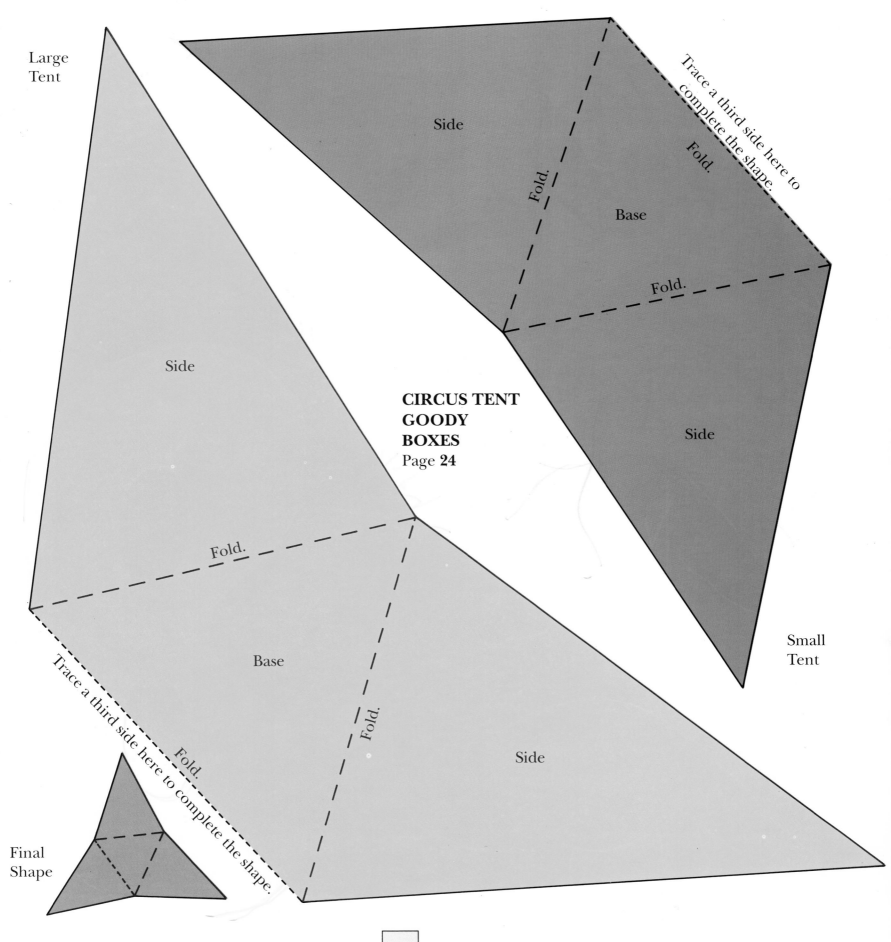

Large
Tent

Side

Trace a third side here to
complete the shape.

Fold.

Side

Fold.

Base

Fold.

CIRCUS TENT
GOODY
BOXES
Page **24**

Side

Fold.

Small
Tent

Trace a third side here to complete the shape.

Fold.

Base

Fold.

Side

Final
Shape

85

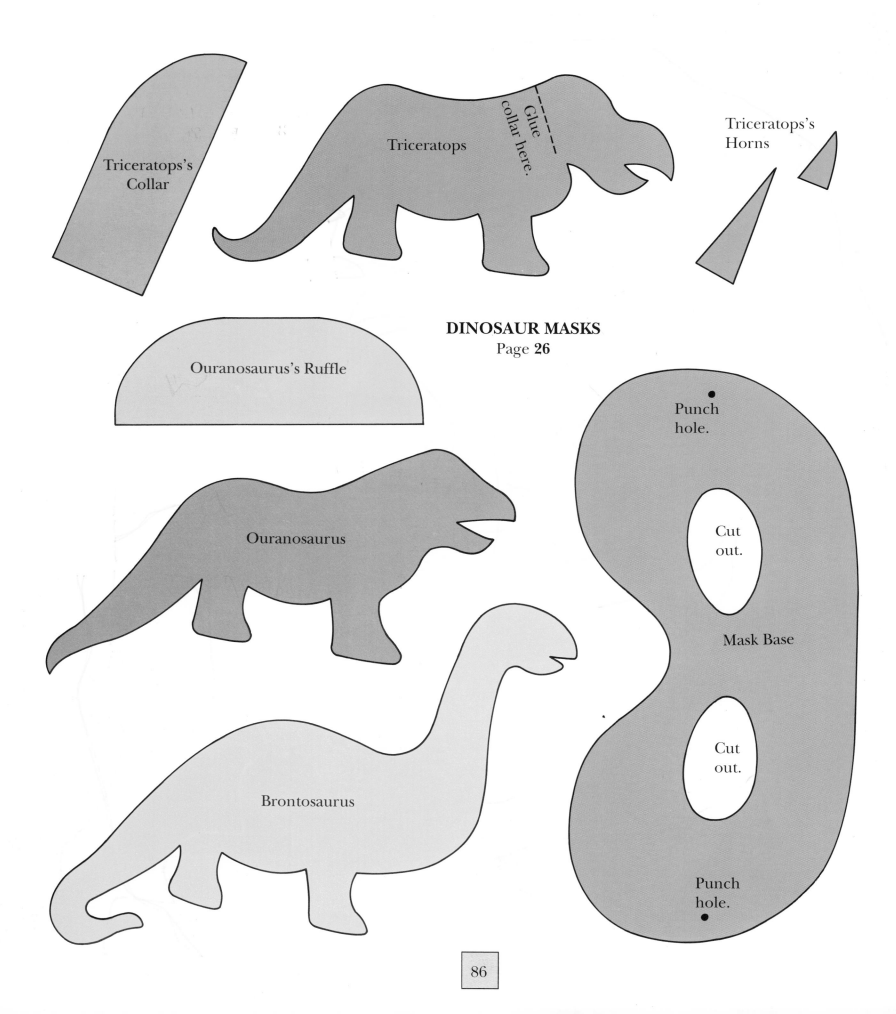

Triceratops's Collar

Triceratops

Glue collar here.

Triceratops's Horns

DINOSAUR MASKS
Page 26

Ouranosaurus's Ruffle

Punch hole.

Cut out.

Ouranosaurus

Mask Base

Cut out.

Brontosaurus

Punch hole.

86

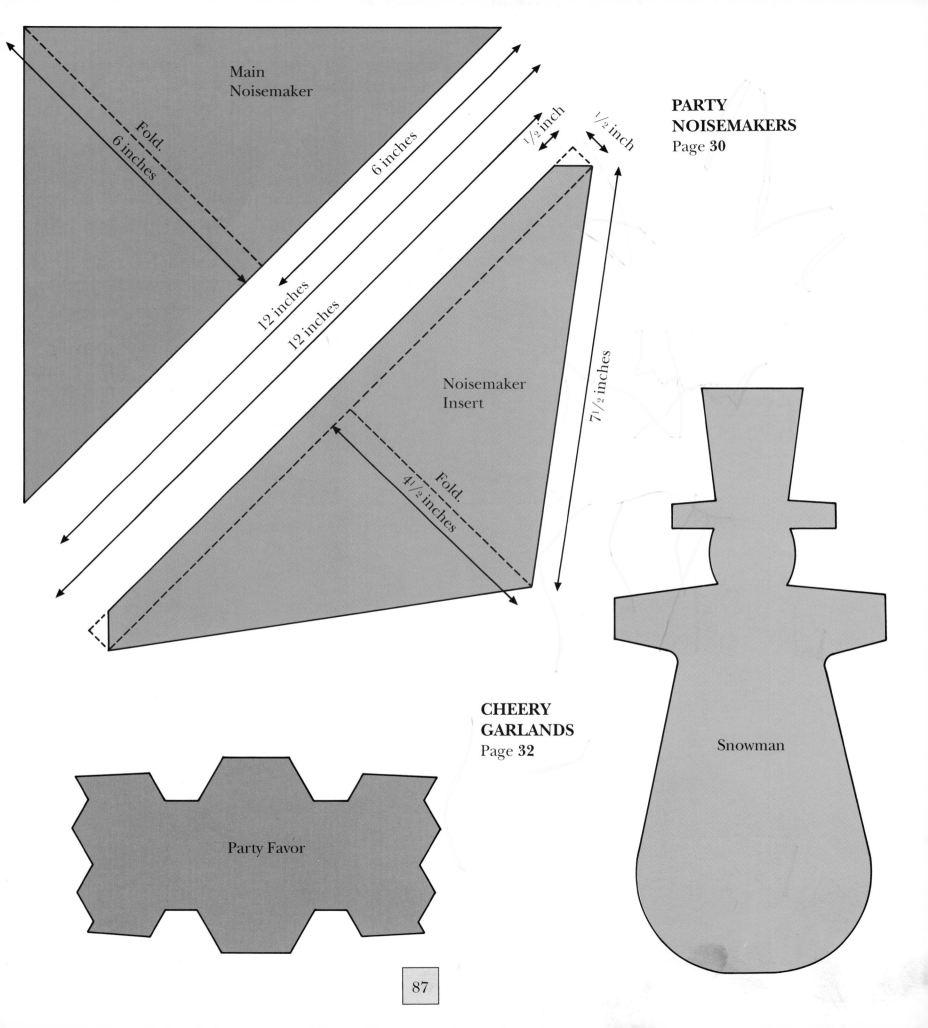

Main
Noisemaker

Fold.
6 inches

6 inches

12 inches

12 inches

½ inch

½ inch

7½ inches

**PARTY
NOISEMAKERS**
Page **30**

Noisemaker
Insert

Fold.
4½ inches

**CHEERY
GARLANDS**
Page **32**

Snowman

Party Favor

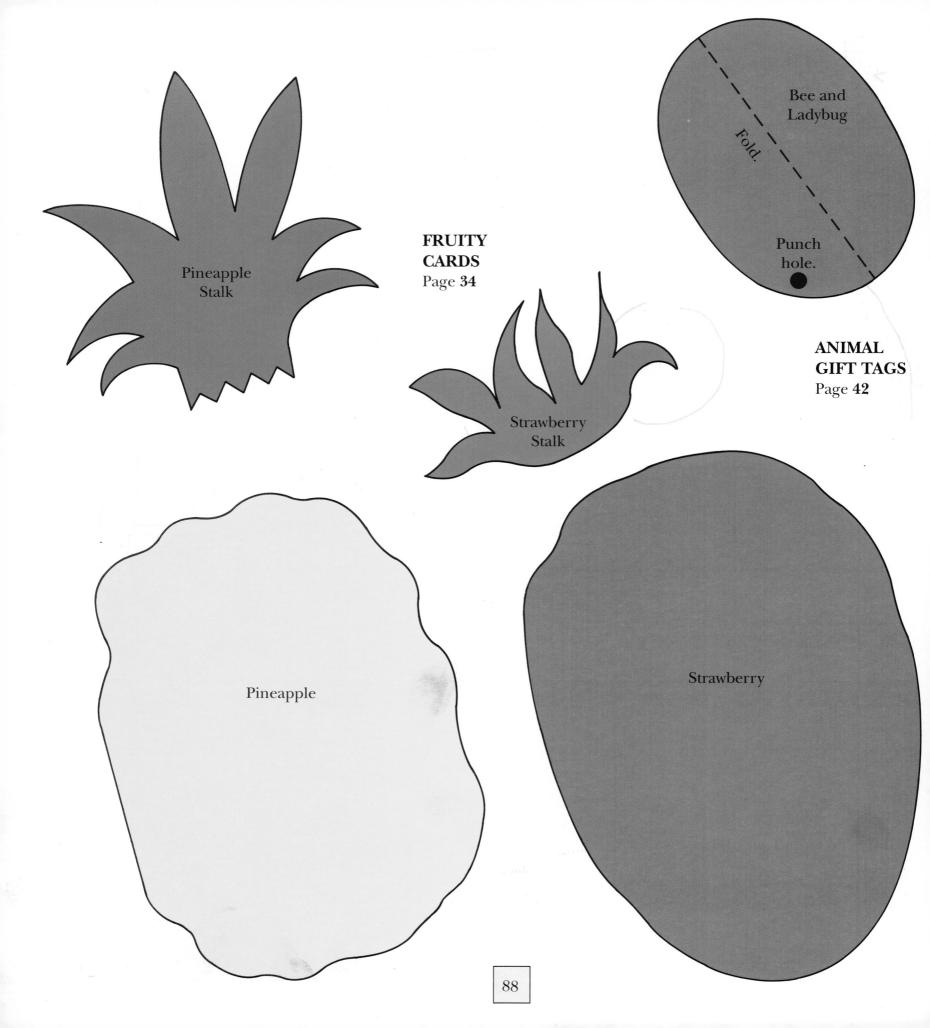

Pineapple
Stalk

**FRUITY
CARDS**
Page **34**

Bee and
Ladybug

Fold.

Punch
hole.

**ANIMAL
GIFT TAGS**
Page **42**

Strawberry
Stalk

Pineapple

Strawberry

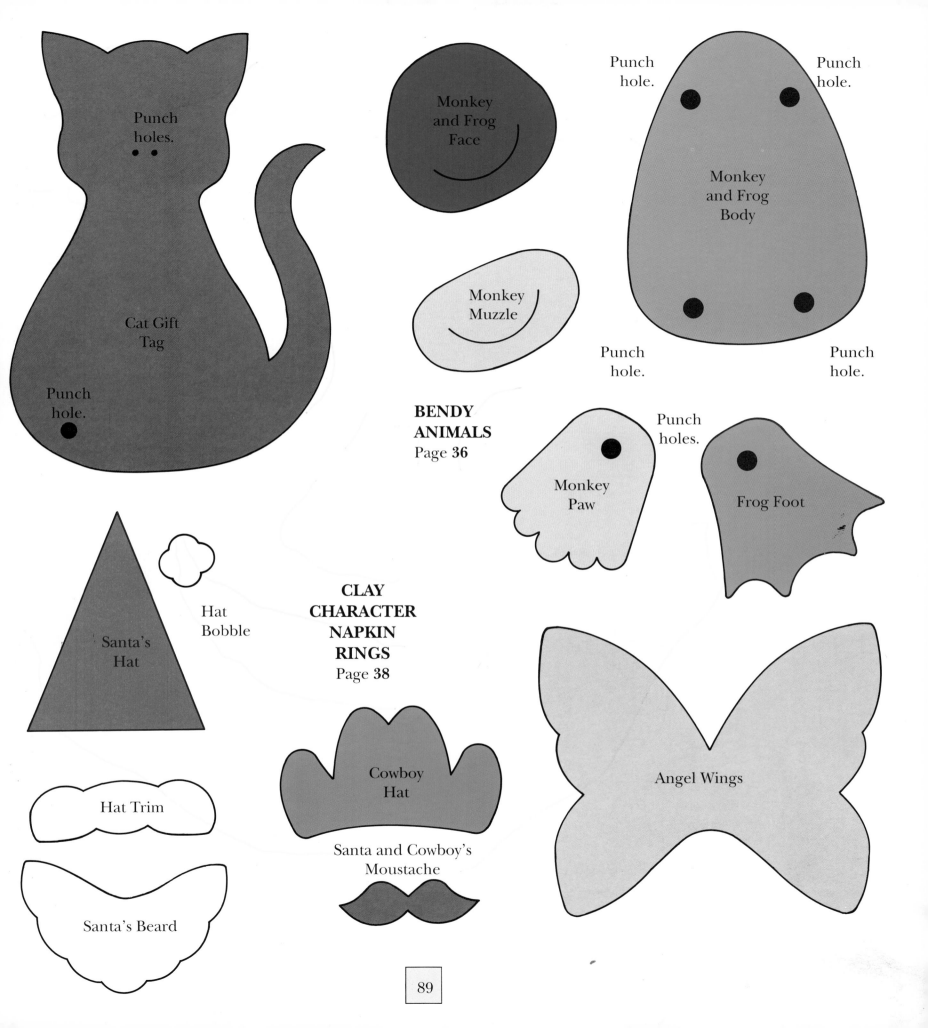

Punch holes.

Cat Gift Tag

Punch hole.

Monkey and Frog Face

Monkey Muzzle

Punch hole.

Punch hole.

Monkey and Frog Body

Punch hole.

Punch hole.

BENDY ANIMALS
Page **36**

Punch holes.

Monkey Paw

Frog Foot

Hat Bobble

Santa's Hat

CLAY CHARACTER NAPKIN RINGS
Page **38**

Cowboy Hat

Hat Trim

Santa and Cowboy's Moustache

Angel Wings

Santa's Beard

89

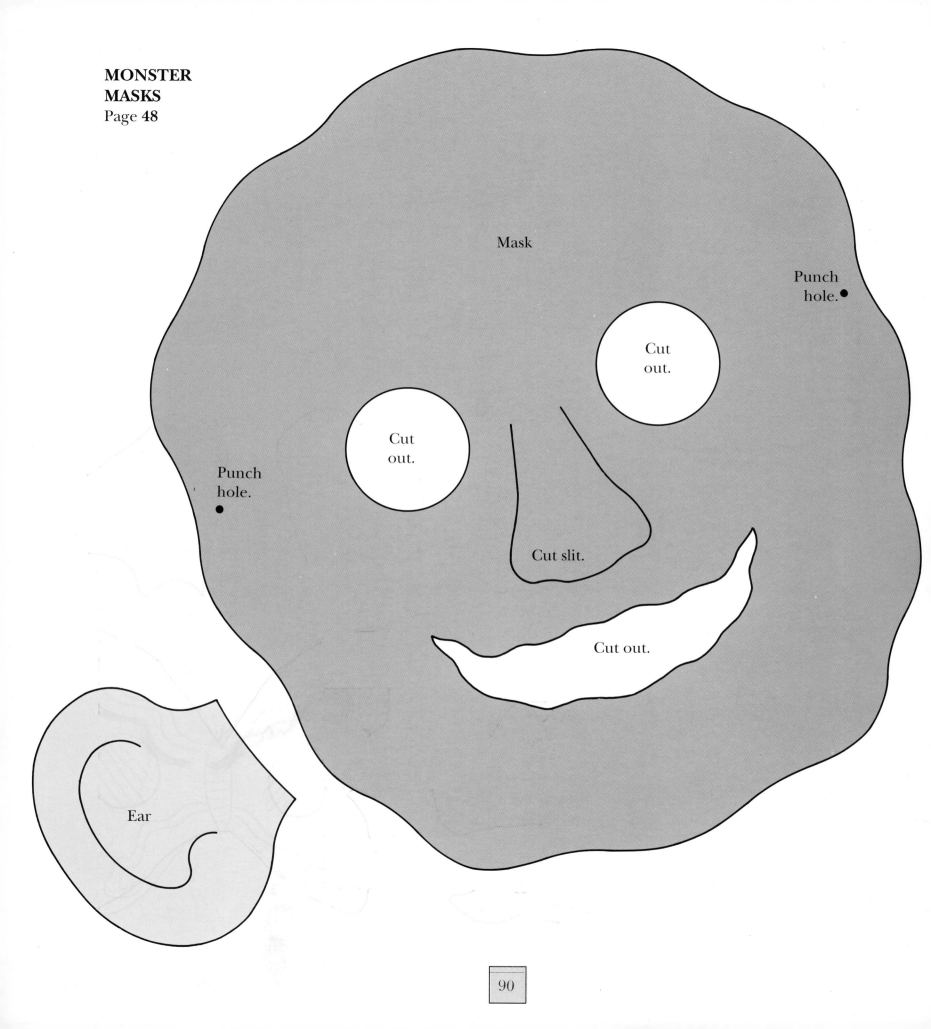

Mask

Punch hole.

Cut out.

Cut out.

Punch hole.

Cut slit.

Cut out.

Ear

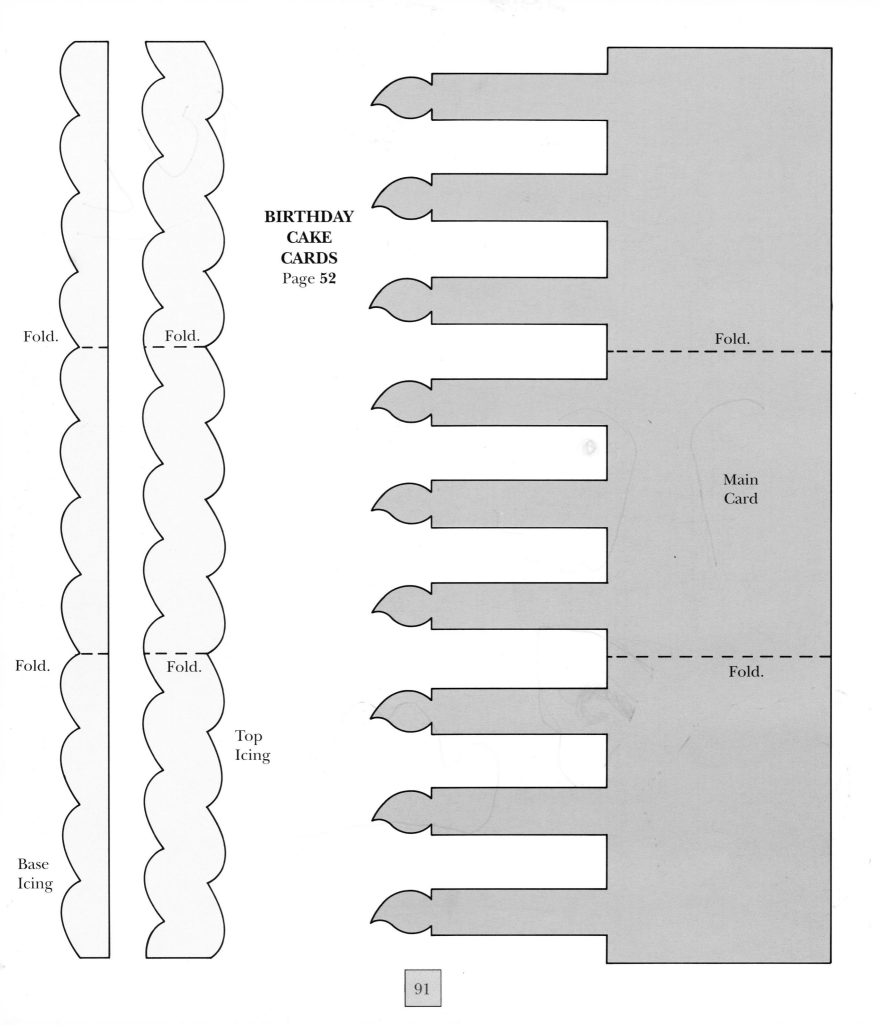

BIRTHDAY CAKE CARDS
Page **52**

Fold.

Fold.

Fold.

Fold.

Main Card

Top Icing

Base Icing

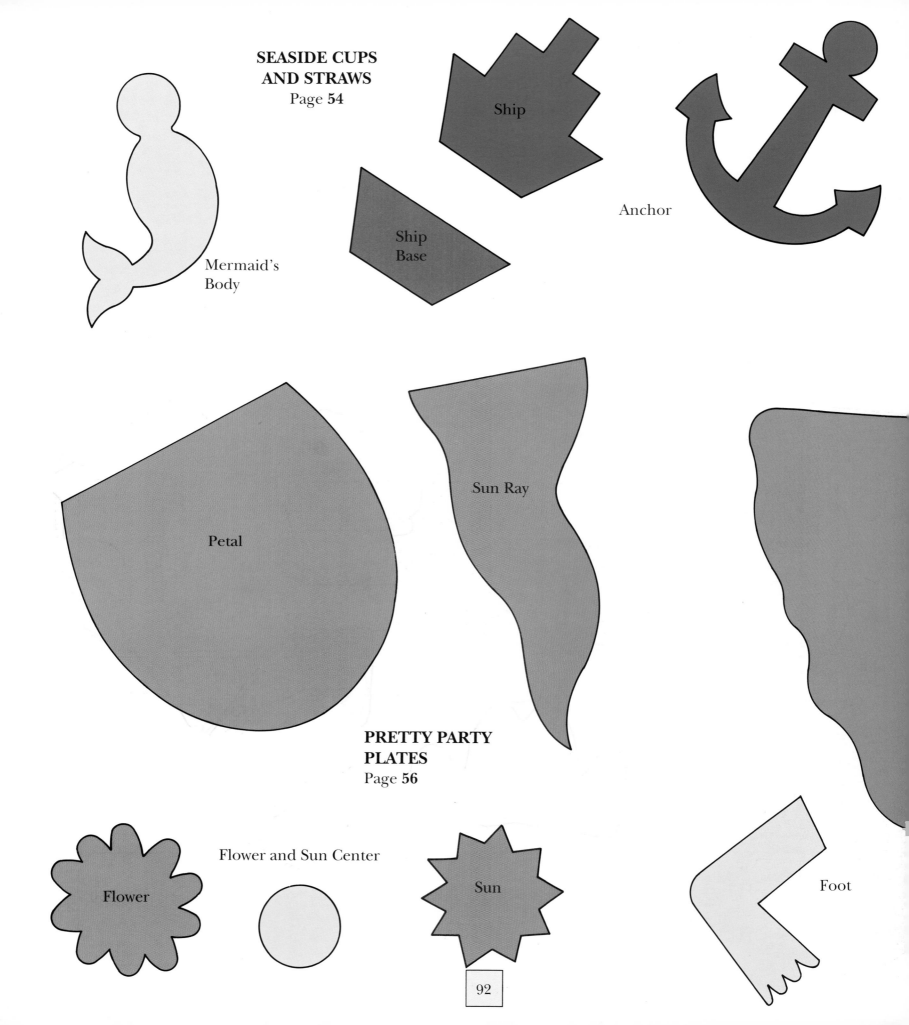

SEASIDE CUPS
AND STRAWS
Page **54**

Ship

Anchor

Mermaid's
Body

Ship
Base

Petal

Sun Ray

PRETTY PARTY
PLATES
Page **56**

Flower and Sun Center

Flower

Sun

Foot

92

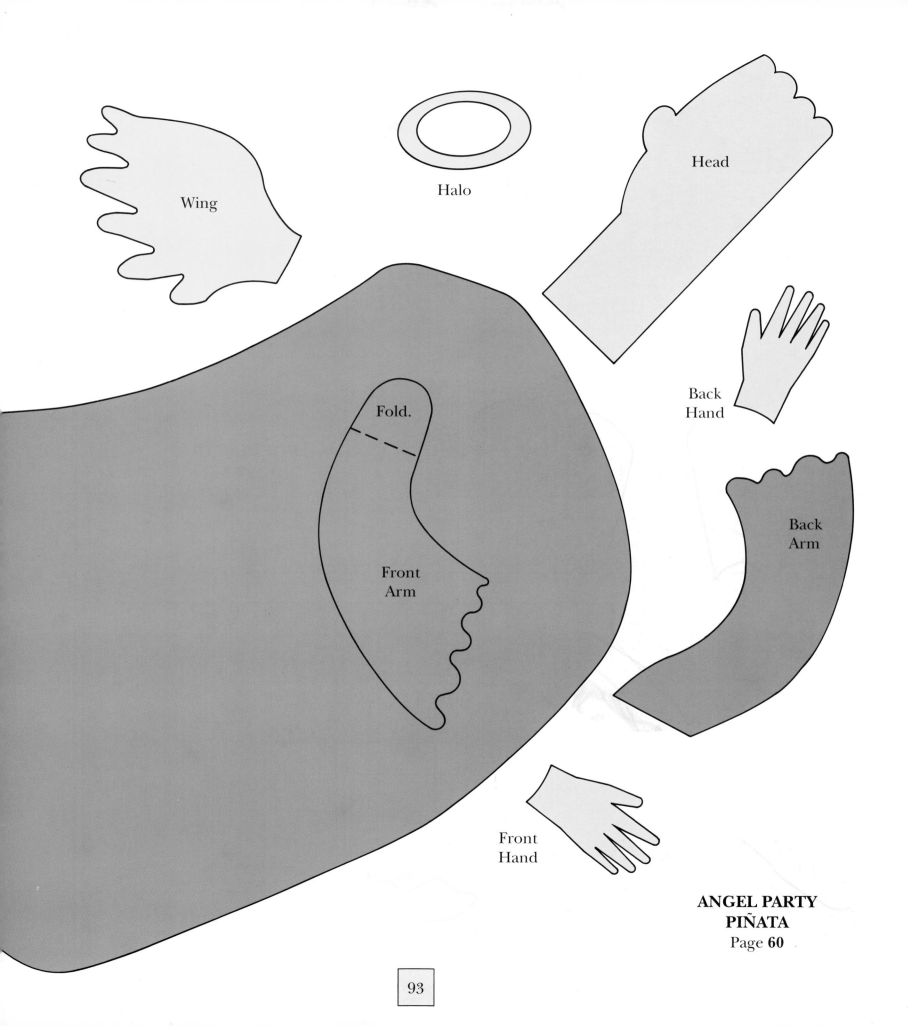

Wing

Halo

Head

Back
Hand

Fold.

Front
Arm

Back
Arm

Front
Hand

**ANGEL PARTY
PIÑATA**
Page **60**

93

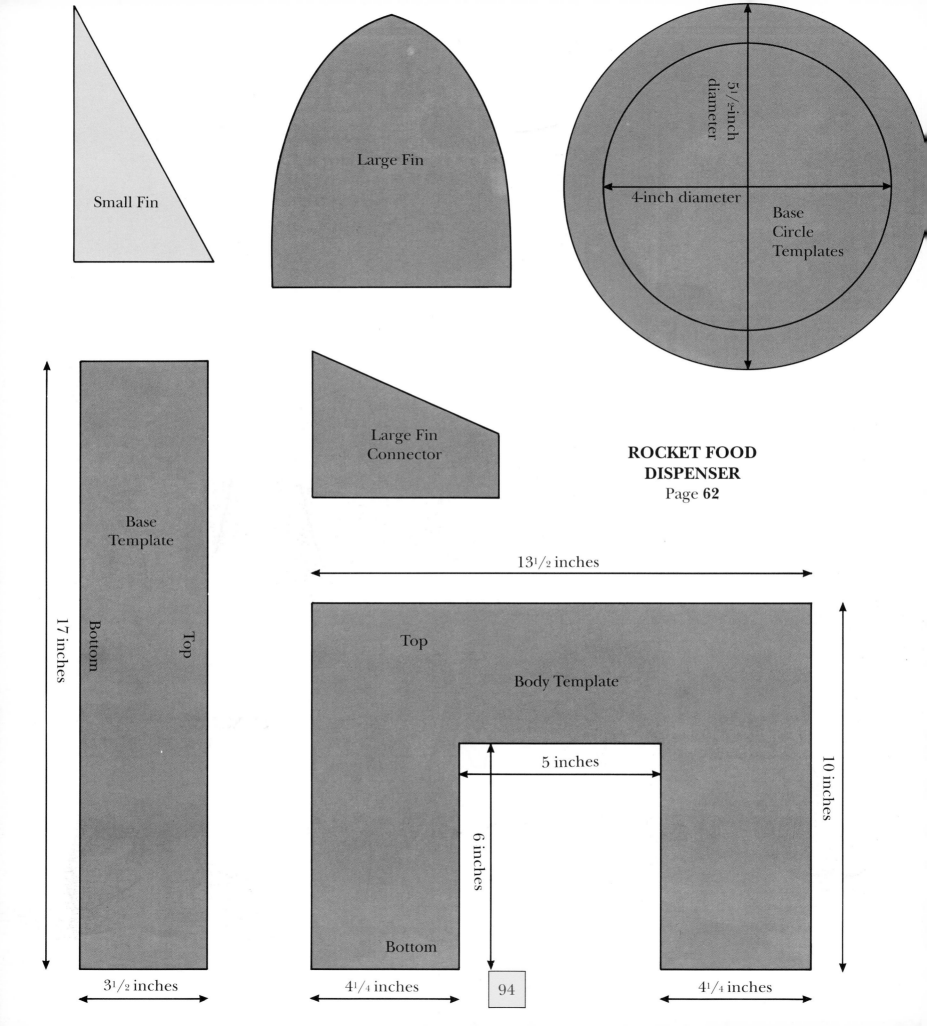

Small Fin

Large Fin

5½-inch diameter

4-inch diameter

Base Circle Templates

Base Template

Bottom

Top

17 inches

3½ inches

Large Fin Connector

ROCKET FOOD DISPENSER
Page **62**

13½ inches

Top

Body Template

5 inches

6 inches

Bottom

10 inches

4¼ inches

4¼ inches

94

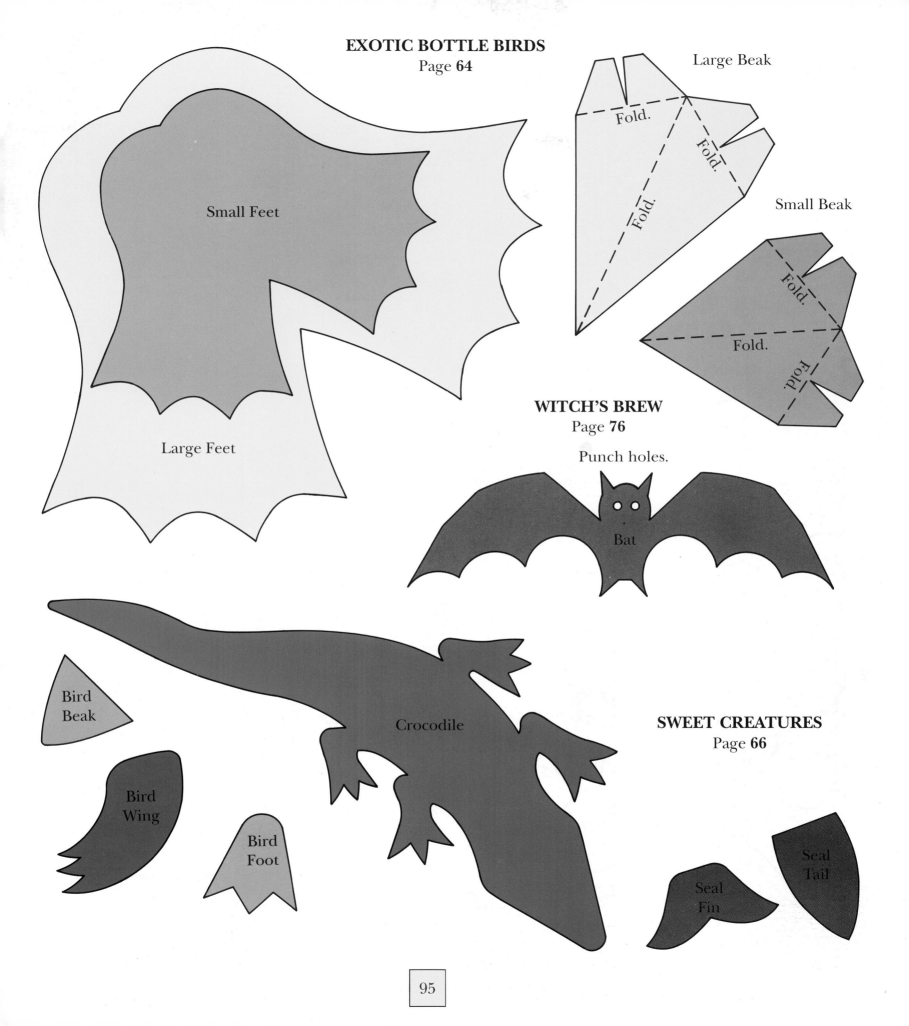

EXOTIC BOTTLE BIRDS
Page **64**

Large Beak

Fold.

Fold.

Fold.

Small Beak

Fold.

Fold.

Fold.

Small Feet

Large Feet

WITCH'S BREW
Page **76**

Punch holes.

Bat

Bird
Beak

Crocodile

SWEET CREATURES
Page **66**

Bird
Wing

Bird
Foot

Seal
Fin

Seal
Tail

INDEX

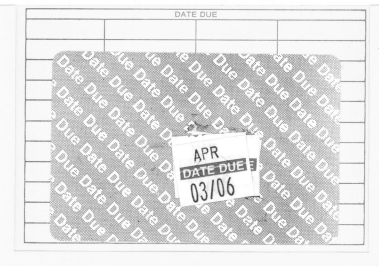